Hollywood North
Creating the Canadian Motion Picture Industry

Hollywood North
Creating the Canadian
Motion Picture Industry

By
Michael Spencer
with
Suzan Ayscough

Cantos International Publishing, Inc.

Published by Cantos International Publishing, Inc.

National Library of Canada Cataloguing in Publication

Spencer, Michael, 1919-

   Hollywood North : Creating the Canadian Motion Picture Industry
   Includes index.
   ISBN 2-89594-007-X

   1. Motion picture industry - Canada - History. 2. Motion picture - Canada - History. 3. Motion picture industry - Quebec (Province) - History. 4. Canada - Cultural policy - History. I. Ayscough, Suzan, 1960-   II. Title.

PN1993.5.C3S63 2003   791.43'0971   C2003-
941365-9

Cover design: Geai Bleu Graphique
Text design and composition: André Chapleau

Cantos International Publishing Inc.
294 square Saint-Louis, 2nd floor
Montreal, Quebec H2X 1A4
Telephone 514-904-2024

Printed and Bound in Canada

10 9 8 7 6 5 4 3 2 1

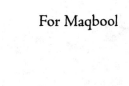

For Maqbool

TABLE OF CONTENTS

FOREWORD
by Donald Sutherland

Robertson Davies said that the difference between Canada and the United States was just a question of frontiers. For the States it was the Wild West and their hero was an outlaw; for Canadians it was the Far North and our hero was a mounted policeman. I don't know whether my hero is a Mountie but for sure it's a sugar maple. This dauntless hero, this Canadian abstraction, is an overwhelming rush that makes my heart pound. It can be identified by the soul of a determined beaver, by the fragile stalwartness of a dory, by the sound of a spring freshet and a radio turned on to the CBC. It is filled with the glory of our undying pursuit of peace; of our willingness to give up our lives to preserve that peace. And it's as funny as W.O. Mitchell and Stephen Leacock and Lorne Michaels all sitting in a room and giggling together. My Canadian hero lives with Lester Pearson and dreams of the United Nations and no matter what language he speaks, no matter what colour or creed he is, no matter where he was born, he's Canadian through and through. It comes from the ground we stand on. It seeps into you and slowly shifts the pattern of your DNA. Hey, we shoot a moose once a year for meat over winter but we don't shoot people, do we?

So, with a nod to Robertson Davies, the American hero is, metaphorically, a gun-toting outlaw, and if you look out your window today you can see that he's spawned many very powerful descendants. Metaphorically, those descendants are what a burgeoning Canadian film industry had to confront in its struggle to exist. This is the story of that battle and it's a truly terrific tale. It was a fierce fight. I was mortally wounded at least three times and pronounced dead twice. Michael Spencer was at the heart of it all, undercover, in the trenches, at the diplomatic level, everywhere. He knows the legions who struggled and he tells the truth. There are no secrets any more. Read on.

Donald Sutherland

FOREWORD
by Carole Laure

In the mid-60s Michael Spencer was a producer at the National Film Board of Canada (NFB). With his colleagues, filmmakers Michel Brault, Denys Arcand, and film commissioner Guy Roberge, he saw that Canadian features needed financial help – government aid to counterbalance the might of the American film industry. A year and a half later, sitting up in the visitor's gallery of the House of Commons in Ottawa, he watched as his dream of a feature film fund was born as the Canadian Film Development Corporation (CFDC). Michael would become its first and longest-serving executive director.

From a young producer at the NFB to his privileged observation post as a completion bonder, he has been one of the country's most astute and active players in the business and the art of film-making.

Michael saw filmmakers as a precious national resource to be developed and sustained, promoted and exported. I would need a chapter of my own here to describe the tour of India that Michael and his beautiful wife, Maqbool, organised for Gilles Carle and me in 1973 to present *La mort d'un bûcheron* and other Canadian films to Indian audiences.

Michael is curious and has been for as long as I've known him. Born in England, he immigrated to Canada at the age of twenty. He wanted to see feature films made that were based on Canadian stories and told by Canadians. He worked tirelessly to convince the government that with a little help, new filmmaking talents would emerge to open a window onto Canada for the rest of the world. He felt strongly that we, as Canadians, would see who we are more clearly through these films. On a financial level he predicted that jobs would be created and that the CFDC would become, in part, self-replenishing.

An industry that is now worth $3 billion a year was well-served by the $10 million the government invested to start up the CFDC, known today as Telefilm Canada.

Here's a great story, told by a lifelong producer and ambassador of Canadian film. Thank you, Michael, for listening and watching and for continuing to speak for us.

Carole Laure

INTRODUCTION

"All censure of a man's self is oblique praise."
— Samuel Johnson

*H*ollywood North — the phrase echoes through the countless newspaper stories and magazine articles written over the years about the Canadian film industry. It's not a location, but a concept: that the success, glamour, and all-American dream of the motion picture industry can be recreated in Canada. Was establishing Hollywood North always the real desire of Canadians? Or did the struggle to develop an independent Canadian feature film industry inadvertently drive us into the arms of our friendly neighbours to the south? For one half of the Canadian feature film industry (the English-speaking half), Hollywood is Mecca, the Holy Grail, the pot of gold at the end of the rainbow. For the other half (the French-speaking half), the idea is to compete with Hollywood films without having to pull your cultural roots out of the ground, to succeed in your own market and then expand around the world.

For most of my career in the Canadian film industry I've been lucky enough to be on both the English and French sides of the action. I could never have done this as a scriptwriter, director, or producer; for that you have to be in one camp or the other. When the Canadian government decided many years ago to provide funds for culture, a cadre of bilingual and bicultural civil servants arrived on the scene. Over the years they acquired the title "cultural bureaucrat" — an oxymoron describing a person who, while sensitive to artistic or intellectual ability, is an ostensibly inflexible or insensitive

1

administrator. This book is about the travails and adventures of one such bureaucrat who set out to achieve an elusive goal: a French and English, Canadian-based feature film industry whose object is not only to entertain but, as all industries should, to contribute to the economy, create jobs, and make money for its investors.

My hope in writing this book is to reach a generation now in film schools who ought to know about how it all began. I caution them, though, that this is an unofficial history, a first-hand observer's view of events. I haven't tried to be objective; I prefer to let my prejudices show. I'm a believer in the idea that if you have to work for a living you should find a job you enjoy. I found two, actually: one as a producer and one as a cultural bureaucrat. I make no apology for a certain lack of gravitas in my writing. I've tended to emphasize the most pleasant aspects of my career (I am in show business, after all!), but I trust that those with whom I had the pleasure of working know that I always took them seriously. Throughout my career, I met hundreds of people. I wish I could remember them all. This book contains my memories of some of them, but there are many more who stayed the course. I salute them.

My good fortune began on Quadra Island, somewhere between Vancouver Island and the mainland. I had been enjoying a holiday with my cousins on that pine-studded island, far away from my home in England, fishing and making trips across the Inside Passage to Campbell River where my uncle John Walker was the magistrate. I was on the island on September 3, 1939, when Neville Chamberlain declared in solemn tones before the British House of Commons that the United Kingdom was now at war with Germany. My life was about to change.

The war, of course, compelled me to find the fastest route back to the U.K. and so I took a train to New York via Chicago hoping to use the return half of my ticket on the USS *Manhattan* that had brought me from Southampton to New York earlier in the summer. But since all sailing had been cancelled due to the war I decided to spend the winter in New York, where I obtained a part-time job at the Museum of Modern Art. It was here that I learned that John Grierson, the pioneer of documentary film, had recently arrived in Ottawa and was setting up the National Film Board of Canada (NFB). I had always wanted to be a filmmaker, so I immediately decided to go there in search of employment. I had been the owner of a 9.5 mm motion picture camera for many years and had always been an enthusiastic moviegoer. While in New York I had made a short film about model railways that I took with me in the hope that it might qualify me for a job.

I was surprised that my interview with Grierson went so well. It was probably because I kept my mouth shut while listening to him talk about the successful German initiative of using cameramen who were part of the Wehrmacht to bring the war to movie theatres. He dreamt of creating an armed services film and photo unit to record the Canadian war effort, and he convinced me that I had a role to play in it. But Grierson was the film commissioner and not a high-ranking military officer, so this idea would have to wait. In the meantime he thought I could be useful at the National Film Board. I became a cameraman and editor there and worked on several documentaries before enlisting in the Canadian armed forces.

Grierson was a surprise passenger on my troopship to the U.K. In his capacity as film commissioner he was hoping to choose the personnel for the first Canadian Army Film Unit then being mobilized in the U.K. Unsurprisingly, the army rejected his nominees, with the exception of myself and a British cameraman. As a staff sergeant and later a captain in the Canadian Army film and photo unit, I served in the U.K., Italy, and Germany. The purpose of the unit was to shoot footage of the Canadian army in action. In that pre-television era, it was all shot in 35 mm black and white and sent to NFB headquarters in Ottawa. From there it went to New York where the Americans produced our biweekly Canadian newsreels. In reality, they were American newsreels with only two or three Canadian stories added.

INTRODUCTION

3

During the fours years I was in the Canadian Army film and photo unit, all my friends were Canadian; I always read *The Maple Leaf*, a newspaper produced by the Canadian Army and full of stories about life in Canada; and I had married an officer in the Canadian Women's Army Corps at the church of St. Martin in the Fields in Trafalgar Square in June 1944. I had, in short, become Canadian and my return to Ottawa was inevitable.

The year I got married Grierson made a second trip to Europe and came to Normandy to see how the film and photo unit operated. I spent an exhilarating day with him in my jeep (I was now a lieutenant) roving around behind the Canadian and the American lines. We eventually reached Mont St-Michel, where I relished Grierson's explanation of the intricacies of the Perpendicular architecture of the abbey there. I had found a friend and a mentor.

I returned to Canada on the *Queen Mary* in the spring of 1945 and began my career anew at the National Film Board. I wanted to make documentary films and considered myself an artist, not a bureaucrat. I didn't have the slightest idea about the feature film industry, especially in Canada. Who would have thought that I'd become the first executive director of the Canadian Film Development Corporation, an agency with the sole purpose of funding a Canadian feature film industry? I had never heard the term *Hollywood North*, and yet in the years to come I'd have a hand in defining it.

CHAPTER 1
CANADIAN CINEMA 101
1945–1964

Late director Claude Jutra rehearses a tender dance moment with an unidentified actress in 1979.

In the early days of the twentieth century, Canada's English-language talents in the movie business — and they were considerable — followed the money to Hollywood. Among the hopefuls were actress Norma Shearer, who abandoned Westmount; star Mary Pickford, who quit Toronto; and Louis B. Mayer, who forsook Saint John to become head of Metro Goldwyn Mayer. These expatriates weren't alone; Hollywood was also attracting the best actors, directors, and writers from England, Germany, France, and Scandinavia (countries with film industries of their own), including Greta Garbo, Ronald Colman, and Ernst Lubitsch.

Hollywood has always attracted global talent and the best scripts. And talent, of course, attracts talent. As Canadian director Norman Jewison once said, "I'll go anywhere there's a good script. It doesn't matter if it's Canada, or Argentina, or Pakistan. I would go anywhere. I consider myself a director. If you have a good script, I'll shoot it."

The food chain of show business is no different today than it was in the last century. The Americans controlled Canadian theatres, and I had never questioned that fact. I never gave any serious consideration to the lack of Canadian features in the theatres. After all, I was working in production at the National Film Board (NFB), which during the 1940s released two series of information shorts every month in these same theatres. NFB documentaries and animation films were known around the world for their quality. I was probably a bit snooty about entertainment films back then.

But all that would soon change. After the war ended in 1945 I resumed my work at the NFB in Ottawa, in the same building on the corner of John and Sussex streets where I had begun my career in October 1940. Chimney Swifts were still nesting just outside the front door of the rundown sawmill building and the postwar NFB was still churning out world-class documentaries. But the NFB itself had changed drastically after the departure of my first Canadian film mentor, film commissioner John Grierson. During the war Grierson had dictated which units were making which documentaries, but now, under Ross McLean, directors and producers were coming up with their own ideas. The titles of the films to be produced would gradually come from them and not from the film commissioner.

My immediate assignment was as an assistant to production secretary James Beveridge. He had no real authority or power, yet had been assigned the formidable task of coordinating the work of the twelve units that Grierson had set up to handle the Board's production program. I was to give Beveridge a hand in dealing with the producers who were increasingly disinclined to concede their own priorities, especially in the sound recording theatres and the film laboratories. It was a job, I would discover, that required diplomatic skills more than production experience.

Since John Grierson had made certain that the NFB was legally responsible for *all* government film activity — every department had to report to the Board about any film business whatsoever — I got a call one day from Archie Newman, the information officer of the Department of Trade and Commerce. He wanted, he said, my assistance on a Canada–U.S. venture called the Canadian Cooperation Project. I thought it was sufficiently important to prepare for the meeting by doing some research on the independent film industry in Canada. What I found out both appalled and intrigued me.

The movie business in English Canada has always revolved around ownership of the theatres, which had been built by Canadian entrepreneurs to distribute American films in such major cities as Vancouver, Toronto, and Montreal. There were some sporadic attempts to produce English-language feature films in Canada, but they encountered opposition from the powerful Motion Picture Association of America (MPAA). One of its early members, Lewis Selznick — father of the more famous David —

set the tone of its paternalistic attitude towards Canada in 1922, the year the MPAA was founded. "If Canadian stories are worthwhile making into films, companies will be sent to Canada to make them," Selznick declared.

In the 1920s there had been a successful Canadian-owned theatre chain called the Allan/First National. It had theatres nationwide and was competing for product with American-owned theatre chains. There was one significant problem: supply. The American chains, especially Famous Players with its contacts in Hollywood, soon cornered the market, forcing Allan/First National theatres into bankruptcy and then buying the chain at fire sale prices.

By 1930 Famous Players had become the largest and most powerful theatre chain in Canada, controlling 207 movie houses. It was effectively making it impossible for the independent theatre owners to do business. The government of Ontario decided that a monopoly existed and took Famous to court under the Combines Investigation Act, alleging that it was using unethical tactics against its competition.

The MPAA was on the case immediately on behalf of its member studio, Paramount. It employed an effective lobbyist, Colonel Cooper, who was instrumental in convincing the Ontario government that it should drop the case. When the government's lawyers suggested during the trial that a 25 percent quota be applied to Ontario theatres in favour of Canadian feature films, the colonel retorted: "The profits of the motion picture industry in Canada are in running theatres, not in the making and distributing of motion pictures." Thus, the idea of an independent Canadian film industry was shot down in flames for the first time.

Clearly, the major U.S. film studios wielded a lot of power over the Canadian film scene. Paramount Pictures, Warner Brothers, Twentieth Century Fox, MGM, et al. had gained effective control of Canadian theatres and distribution companies in the 1930s and weren't about to give it up.

Armed with this background information, I went to the meeting with Archie Newman. The Canadian Cooperation Project had been put in place a year or so before, and Newman wanted the NFB's help in preparing the statistics he needed in order to report on it. But the project, as I had suspected, was a camouflage. The deal, cooked up by J.J. Fitzgibbons (the head of Famous) and the gurus at Maclaren's (an advertising agency in Toronto), was ostensibly an offer to "promote tourism to Canada" in American theatres. But in reality it was designed to ward off the threat of exchange controls on their Canadian box office revenues. In other words, it was a way to ensure that American profits from exhibition and distribution money would continue to flow to the Hollywood studios. Incredibly, C.D. Howe, the powerful minister of Trade and Commerce (known familiarly as Canada's Minister of Everything), fell for it.

According to the deal, shorts would be produced and distributed in the U.S. to promote tourism to Canada, and more stories about Canada would appear in U.S. newsreels. Added to this was the provision that the MPAA would employ someone in Hollywood to visit the script departments of all the major studios and propose that the names of Canadian cities and provinces be referred to as often as possible. If a script had a character who talked about Peoria or Sioux Falls or Pittsburgh, why not make that Edmonton, Toronto, or Halifax? American tourists would theoretically flock to these places when they heard of them in Hollywood movies.

But the NFB was already distributing films and newsreel stories in the U.S., and very successfully, too. Now all this activity was to be reported back to Howe as the result of the CCP. It was humiliating to have the Department of Trade and Commerce take credit for the work of the NFB. And the worst part was that the Canadian government was so impressed by this crazy scheme that it had decided not to impose any controls on Canadian box office receipts at all.

I never heard of any Canadian benefit from the CCP, which was allowed to die of embarrassment a few years later, but it served its purpose for the MPAA, since there was no interruption in the flow of money back to the U.S. And the majors learned another lesson: they made sure that their top people in Canada kept their contacts warm. An archival internal document from the 1950s underlines the point: "Bob Winters [the new minister of Trade and Commerce] as you very likely know is as swell a guy as Mike Pearson. We both got to know him pretty well and sewed him up tight on the project. We will certainly have a very strong man in our corner . . . for any future matter which might need help and understanding from the Canadian Government." The writer is unknown but the message is clear.

By the early 1950s the anti-communist McCarthy era had arrived and the Cold War trenches were being dug in Washington. The fallout was felt in Canada as the federal government became increasingly uneasy with the NFB, which was accused in the press of employing too many left-wing staff members.

I had been promoted to producer in charge of the film unit responsible for all government departments. Most departments were opposed to the clause in the National Film Act that gave the NFB control of all government film production (including processing), and this was especially true of the Department of National Defence. Reports in the press were the perfect excuse for Defence to inform me that they could disregard the National Film Act for security reasons; all their film processing was now to be done by Ottawa-based Crawley Films. Questions were soon being raised in the House of Commons about this breach of the Act. The resulting controversy led the government to ask for the resignation of film commissioner Ross McLean and to appoint the editor of *Maclean's* magazine, W. Arthur Irwin, to replace him.

Irwin's first small task was to sort out this "communist" security threat. In those days, as in these, matters of security were handled by the RCMP, whose role was to provide reports on any activities of government employees that might compromise national security. Irwin proceeded immediately to review all the files at the RCMP (there were more than a hundred), and eventually decided that three people should be asked to resign. Irwin then asked me to take on the additional role of the Board security officer. As the producer for National Defence, I was the logical choice. From then on I was required to review all applications for jobs in Production and Technical Services to determine whether or not the applicant posed a security problem.

Sexual deviations, if known or suspected, were often brought to my attention by the RCMP on the assumption that I would not recommend such people for employment. They were "susceptible to blackmail." (I'm not sure on what basis the police thought there was a connection between sexual deviation and disloyalty to the country.) On the other hand, I was also under pressure to look the other way where genuine creative ability was involved.

Fortunately, the final decision always rested with a senior government official at the deputy minister level. In my case, that was Arthur Irwin. As a magazine editor Irwin well knew the importance of talent, and wasn't about to let the RCMP determine who was on his staff. The NFB depended on the quality of its creators to maintain its reputation as one of the best-known film production organizations on the planet. Certainly, the production staff considered themselves an elite; Norman McLaren, Colin Low, Roman Kroitor, Gerald Potterton, and Donald Brittain had worldwide reputations. The rest of us, in their shadow, felt superior, too. Needless to say, we rarely paid attention to what the RCMP were telling us.

Irwin's real mission became the NFB's move from Ottawa to Montreal. He was from Toronto and had the usual Torontonian's mistrust for the city of Ottawa. It was not, after all, the dynamic, creative centre of the country. Irwin also realized that it would be difficult to get Quebec producers to work there. The sawmill on the Rideau River was obviously inadequate, and ugly to boot. So Irwin found the perfect excuse: the building held an enormous amount of explosive nitrate film . . . a spectacular explosion just waiting to happen. New premises obviously had to be built, and preferably not in Ottawa.

The roots of the Canadian feature film industry had already been planted in Montreal at the turn of the century. Leo-Ernest Ouimet opened his first "ouimetoscope," as he liked to call his movie theatres, in Montreal in 1906. By mid-century there were a number of active film people in the city, including Joseph Alexandre Desève — whose France Film was the major theatre chain in Quebec — and Paul l'Anglais, the most successful producer of the day. Among the Quebec hits l'Anglais produced in that era were director Paul Gury's *Un homme et son péché* (1949), followed by his *Séraphin* (1950) (remade into one film by Charles Binamé in 2002). Other memorable films include *Forbidden Journey* (1950), directed by Richard Jarvis, and Jean-Yves Bigras's *La petite aurore, l'enfant martyre* (1951), which became one of Quebec cinema's greatest successes in that decade. In English Canada, meanwhile, virtually no homegrown feature production was happening. The obvious new home for the NFB was Montreal.

There was some discussion in the newspapers as to whether the NFB should abandon the nation's capital, but the matter was settled when Ottawa's Conservative mayor Charlotte Whitton came out publicly against the move. Her intervention backfired: it irritated Liberal prime minister Louis St. Laurent, and so had the effect of speeding up the approval process for the move to Montreal, which was finally completed in 1956.

The Montreal studios are still the NFB's home, and have proved flexible enough to remain up to date in 2003, even though some of the facilities are now rented to the private sector. Since the sound stages are under the flight path of a major runway of the Dorval international airport, the ceiling had to be specially soundproofed during construction. It's good to know that Canadian engineers were on top of the technology of soundproofing fifty years ago. No shooting days in the studio have ever been lost because of planes taking off and landing.

The NFB's move to Montreal had the serendipitous effect of boosting Canada's feature film prospects. The fancy new building on Côte-de-Liesse — its state-of-the-art processing laboratory, sound recording studios, and shooting stage were as large and sophisticated as any in Hollywood — immediately attracted a cadre of talented Quebec filmmakers who were anxious to get their hands on the tools of their trade. Many just borrowed its equipment, or profited from the availability of the lab. It was a veritable explosion. And with Board technicians moonlighting on Quebec features, at night the place was humming.

The NFB's modern production facilities even seduced a number of Quebec filmmakers into joining the staff, including those who would go on to give Canada its international reputation — Gilles Carle, Denys Arcand, and Claude Jutra. Whereas Jutra started by working with Norman McLaren, Arcand says he got there almost by accident:

> I was originally hired because I had just finished my master's degree in history. When I joined the NFB in '61, there was no *feature* film industry whatsoever: the only place you could make films was the NFB. So at least on the Quebec side, everybody was there. Outside the Film Board there was nothing: it was a vast desert. Really nothing! The feature movement slowly evolved because people joined the Film Board, in fact, for the wrong reasons. They really wanted to make feature films but the Film Board wasn't doing feature films. So they slowly tried to push the Film Board into doing lengthier films, bigger films, eventually feature films.

Denis Héroux was a theatre student who wanted to use university money (earmarked for a stage production) to make a movie. The University of Montreal had promised $15,000 for the next student production and Héroux snared it for his film *Seul ou avec d'autres*. (The title, he explained, is drawn from a Catholic priest's routine response to an admission of sin during confession.) Héroux secured Michel Brault as cameraman, thanks to some serious chutzpah and a newspaper article that led Héroux to call Brault at the NFB. "The papers say you're the best cameraman in the world!" Héroux exclaimed. "Who are you?" Brault asked. "And what do you want?" "I'm a student," Héroux said. "I want to make a movie and I want you to be the cameraman." Brault invited him to meet the boys at the NFB. Pierre Juneau, then director of French production, okayed the use of the Board's equipment for the project, because it was used on "Michel's production." The film got made, and was entered in the Semaine de la critique in Cannes on a whim and a prayer. Marie-José Raymond, its star, was the first Canadian actress to cause a stir on the terrace at the Carleton Hotel in Cannes.

A.W. Trueman succeeded Arthur Irwin as film commissioner in 1953, and wanted to promote me to head of the Liaison Division. This was the crunch: did I want to be a producer or a bureaucrat? But I had always followed the precept of never refusing a promotion, so that day in Trueman's office I made the decision to stay in Ottawa to handle the relations between the Board's producers in Montreal and the various government departments in Ottawa. It was this choice that would determine my career in the development of the Canadian feature film industry.

My new assignment took me regularly to Montreal. I became familiar with all the film action there, including the first Montreal International Film Festival in 1960, at which the uncensored version of Alain Resnais's *Hiroshima, mon amour* took Quebec cinephiles by storm. By the time the film was set to open in theatres later that fall the censor board had chopped about fifteen minutes out of it — and Quebecers took to the streets. Rock Demers, who was to become a famous Quebec producer, remembers that "because so many people had seen it at the festival, there was a big protest in the street with banners . . . with everything." The protest "was strong enough to have the Quebec government form a committee to study the rules of censorship." And so it was that in 1963 André Guerin was named president of Quebec's censor board and replaced censorship with a classification system. In no time, Quebec had the most liberal standards in North America, and Montreal had arrived on the world film scene.

Montreal was a bustling metropolis compared with the more sedate Ottawa. I happily fell into a routine of taking the train to Montreal every Thursday morning and returning on the weekend.

On today's VIA trains everyone sits working on their laptop computers and chatting on their cell phones rather than with fellow passengers. But in those days the atmosphere on the CP train was that of a rather exclusive club. During the first-class breakfast (complete with lots of heavy silver cutlery and uniformed waiters) I often had interesting conversations with my fellow passengers; I once even found myself chatting with Lord Douglas Home, who at the time was prime minister of the U.K. — and, like me, a bird-watcher, so we had things to talk about. Morning meetings at the NFB in Ville St. Laurent with producers were followed by luncheon gossip in the Bernard Tavern. Then I'd taxi downtown to a French restaurant for dinner (always excellent, this being Montreal) with director Donald Brittain before heading out to the infamous nightclubs. I became quite an aficionado of these risqué spectacles (which were probably not as revealing as they are today — but the dancing was just as suggestive). Our evenings invariably continued into the wee hours, resulting in a heavy hangover when I awoke in the LaSalle Hotel on Stanley Street. But I prided myself on being bright-eyed and bushy-tailed upon arrival at the office the next morning. I soon found myself looking forward to my weekly "business trip" to swingin' Montreal.

While some Quebec filmmakers became NFB staff members, others were pursuing their dreams of producing features for entertainment in the private sector; a dream that I supported. By now I had come to believe that the future of the film industry in Canada would need a broader base than the NFB's Grierson-inspired educational mandate.

Cooperatio was one of the first production companies launched on the risky venture of producing features on a shoestring budget. I thought this was a step in the right direction for the private sector; Cooperatio could play a significant role in the future of the Quebec film industry. Its founders — Pierre Patry, Roger Blais, and Jean-Claude Lord — each personally put up $2,000 to buy the raw stock. In those days that was a lot of money! (The Canadian Kodak

Company, the only provider of raw stock, insisted on cash upfront.) Cooperatio's first film was *Trouble-fête* in 1964, a story about a student revolution in a Quebec school. I asked a friend in the camera department if they could "borrow" some equipment. The risky venture turned out to be worthwhile this time, as the film did well in the theatres. Patry later went on to produce *Poussière sur la ville* by Arthur Lamothe and *Entre la mer et l'eau douce* by Michel Brault.

As head of the NFB's Liaison Division I was responsible for supervising the work when a department used the services of private-sector producers. The funds would go directly from the department to the private producer concerned, which meant less money for the NFB's own production division. And so I ended up being squeezed between the NFB and the private sector: both claimed they needed the money. But since many government departments wanted to use the private-sector producers, I was in a good position to assess their potential. The sheer quality of the films and the enthusiasm of the producers convinced me that the private sector could make a contribution to the film scene in Canada.

The Association of Motion Picture Producers and Laboratories of Canada (AMPPLC), which had been founded several years before, was the first effective lobbying group to tackle the NFB. The AMPPLC felt that not giving production work to the private sector was unfair, and so did the information officers of some departments. Since I was sympathetic to what I considered to be the private sector's just demands, they saw me as neutral, possibly even a friend, and so invited me to their meetings. It was in this way that I became acquainted with many of the colourful entrepreneurs who would eventually form the cadre of producers in the emerging Canadian feature film industry.

CHAPTER 2
THE FEDS STEP IN
1957–1963

Guy Roberge.the Government Film Commissioner and Chairman of the National Film Board who gave the Canadian feature film industry meaningful support is seen here with his wife Marie.

The launching of the Canadian feature film industry in the 1960s owed much of its impetus to Guy Roberge, who in 1957 was the first French Canadian named NFB chairman and film commissioner. Roberge, who had been secretary of the Royal Commission on Arts, Letters and Sciences, arrived at his post already well tuned in to the Canadian cultural establishment. As a Quebecer he also had an innate understanding of French culture. This gave him a uniquely dual perspective that would serve him well in the issues he would face during his appointment.

The first major crisis Roberge encountered was the death of Donald Mulholland in 1959. Appointed director of production by Arthur Irwin before the Film Board moved to Montreal, Mulholland had been, in effect, the chief executive of the NFB. His death marked the end of an era. Roberge, who had to put in place a new executive team to deal with both the French and the English, chose to promote Grant McLean as director of English production and Pierre Juneau as director of French production. While retaining my role as head of the Liaison Division, I was also named director of planning, which meant that I would be responsible for the program of the films to be produced by the Board's production units.

In the meantime I had completed my own move from Ottawa to Montreal with my family and was now ensconced in a home in Hampstead. Since it wasn't far from the NFB I decided I could easily get there on my bicycle, an ancient CCM without gears and a brake operated by jamming the pedals backwards. My route took me through back streets, past fancy suburban mansions, and across the Trans-Canada Highway until I ended up at the Board's new premises in St. Laurent. I felt quite good about arriving at this brand-new studio complex on my old bicycle and then proceeding

21

to my large office with a hand-polished boardroom table and desk to match.

I soon discovered, however, that McLean and Juneau insisted on doing their own planning, and that my job involved simply eliminating any duplication between the two plans. Not a very challenging assignment: a director of planning with no planning to do.

When McLean was out of town one of the administrative tasks that fell to me was handling complaints about the cafeteria. When filmmaker Claude Fournier complained that the food wasn't the gourmet fare that he expected to find in a government cafeteria, I duly informed the cafeteria management. But food was obviously not the issue. As far as the administration and operations were concerned, the English were in the majority; the Quebec members of the staff hence felt compelled to keep us on our toes. This was a real problem on Côte-de-Liesse. My lack of conversational French didn't help matters, nor did my lack of contacts in French production.

Since I wasn't in the loop I knew nothing about director Gilles Carle and producer Jacques Bobet's plans to shoot *La vie heureuse de Leopold Z* as a feature. I had approved it on the program as a short about snow clearing in Montreal. But the film, starring Guy L'Ecuyer as Leopold Z and photographed by Jean-Claude Labrecque, went on to break box office records in Quebec. It remains a classic Quebec comedy, and is still often seen on late-night TV, but it was originally camouflaged as a documentary in order to get the paperwork through the English-dominated approval system. Many years later, I had the privilege of introducing Gilles Carle at a gala event in Ottawa when he received a Governor General's Award for his contribution to the film industry in Canada. I reminded the black-tie audience that Carle's first foray into feature film production had been an "illegal operation." For years it had been a feather in Carle's cap that he had duped the NFB's management so easily.

Roberge used the energy of Carle's subterfuge film and its box office success to support his plans for feature films. He would often run into Carle, Michel Brault, Denys Arcand, and other directors in the corridors of the NFB building, and they never missed an opportunity to ask him when he was going to do something officially for feature film production. Aware of my interest in developing the private sector, Roberge confided in me about the momentum building among filmmakers and talked about his ideas. I shared his enthusiasm and had ideas of my own. Roberge and I felt strongly that the producers outside the NFB also merited financial government support, and we were just waiting for an excuse to bring the subject up with the government. He soon realized that he could further the cause of feature film production by convincing the federal government to set up a special fund to finance them.

It was the Conservatives' defeat in the 1963 federal election that opened the door. Roberge, who had once been a Liberal member of the Quebec National Assembly, was now in the position to wield influence among his friends in Lester B. Pearson's newly elected Liberal government.

Roberge asked me to write a letter to the AMPPLC outlining our idea for a special fund for features. The idea was to convince its members, who were in the television commercial business and making information films, that they had a rosy future in feature films. The hidden agenda here was to try to direct their energies into feature film production and keep them off the Board's back so that it could continue to enjoy its control of government film production.

Not all the members of the AMPPLC were in favour, but Roberge had a strong ally in Nat Taylor, who was president of Twentieth Century Theatres and owner of the Toronto International Studios. Taylor had been a vocal supporter of Canadian features for many years. As well as writing a weekly column in the *Canadian Film Weekly* (which he controlled), he was a tireless lobbyist, submitting briefs to federal ministers in support of film production in Canada. "If Canada is to have a feature film industry," he wrote in one issue, "the following goals should be set":

- The eventual employment of thousands of skilled and

highly paid technicians and other people of various talents;

• The export of the fruits of our talent rather than the talent itself, which should result in the return to Canada of millions of dollars of foreign currency annually;

• The creation of a favourable and vivid image of Canada to tens of millions of people throughout the world to the end that our industry and export trade will be greatly benefited.

He was convinced that every one of these goals was attainable. "We shall have a production industry in Canada, and a good thriving one if our government ever gets round to extending a helping hand", he wrote in the February 10, 1960 edition of *Canadian Film Weekly*.

Taylor was associated with Julian Roffmann, who had produced many excellent documentaries for the NFB. Under Taylor's influence, Roffmann had resisted the brain drain of creative Canadian filmmakers heading to Hollywood. He had served as a war correspondent with the Canadian army in Europe, and was actively honing his filmmaking skills via the production of television commercials. But Roffmann also wanted to make a feature film. The story he had in mind (and eventually made in 1961) was entitled *The Mask* and was to be made in 3-D. At the time, Roffmann and Taylor were the only significant producers in English Canada who wanted to get into features.

To get the ball rolling, I asked Roberge to invite Taylor to a meeting of the NFB, where he elaborated on his proposal for Canadian feature film production outlined in *Canadian Film Weekly*. He argued that a Canadian feature film industry was perfectly feasible, and viable, given some government help.

At a subsequent meeting, Roberge convinced the NFB — even some opposed senior executives — to back feature film production through the clause in the Film Act that gives it a responsibility to advise the government on film matters "in the national interest." Ultimately, Roberge persuaded them that the Film Act could include "entertainment." But his real stroke of genius was buried in another strategy: co-production treaties with foreign countries. He was convinced that an international stamp of approval would increase our credibility with our own government (like many things Canadian that get their stamp of approval from a foreigner first). A way had to be found to involve Canadian producers in international co-productions.

Under a co-production treaty, two countries could authorize the production of films involving creators and technical facilities from both nations. The films then had two nationalities and took advantage of government aid from both countries.

France had signed co-production treaties with other European countries as far back as the 1930s, when the export of American entertainment films had begun to make a significant dent in European theatrical distribution. By 1922, when the MPAA was created, most countries had quotas in place to give their own producers a fighting chance in the face of the well-organized American production and distribution business. But could a country like ours, with a limited output of features, use this route?

Roberge had excellent contacts in the Canadian embassy in Paris. He asked our cultural attaché, an old friend of his, to approach the Centre national de la cinématographie on our behalf. The head of the Centre at the time was Michel Fourré-Cormeray, a distinguished civil servant willing to extend France's many co-production treaties to North America. The Centre obligingly sent us a draft treaty, which we found we could easily agree to. After one or two drafts went back and forth, we were invited to go to Paris in March 1963 for the official signing. My fondest memory wasn't the signing itself — a routine affair — but the excellent lunch hosted by Fourré-Cormeray for the Canadian delegation, which included Guy Roberge and Raymond Marie Léger, the head of the NFB's office in Paris who had been instrumental in helping with the paperwork. The lunch was given in a famous restaurant on the Champs-Elysées, where we found ourselves happily seated on a veranda

25

overlooking a beautiful, blooming garden. It had been a cold winter and this was the first warm day of the year.

After Paris came London. Roberge had decided to feel out the situation in the U.K., which at that time, given the opposition of the powerful studio technicians' union, had no co-production agreements with any countries. We had nonetheless been invited to meet with the Producers Association. Our delegation included Taylor, Roffmann, Roberge, and Budge Crawley, a prominent documentary producer who dreamt of making feature films. We rolled out all the arguments for doing co-productions with British producers and laid great stress on our technical facilities, our creative talent, our Rocky Mountains and other spectacular locations, and our enthusiasm to get into feature film production. At the conclusion of the general session we had made what we thought was a compelling presentation about the potential of Canadian feature film production. Then we heard a voice from somewhere in the back, which turned out to be from Robert Clark, a very important U.K. distributor and the head of ABC, a major cinema chain there. When he rose to speak the room fell silent: "Have you got the money?" he said in a broad Scottish accent. This was, of course, exactly what we did not have.

Undeterred, we pressed on. In those days the major European feature film producers were in both France and Italy, so while Roberge headed home I travelled to Rome with Roffman and Crawley to meet the officials of the Italian Ministry responsible for co-production. This was a courtesy call intended to open doors for future negotiations (not to mention a good opportunity for sightseeing). Jules Léger, who later became the Governor General, was then the Canadian ambassador in Rome; Donald Buchanan, whom Crawley and I had known for years, was also living in the city at the time. (Buchanan had been employed by John Grierson in setting up the NFB's distribution system in the 1940s and later became the director of the National Gallery in Ottawa.) It was this fortuitous combination of Léger and Buchanan that resulted in an unintentionally amusing evening.

Buchanan had invited us all over to his palatial apartment for dinner, during which Crawley and I were treated to a game of "oenophile one-upmanship." Léger arrived with three vintage bottles of Italian wine, each of which was carefully uncorked and poured out for a taste. Buchanan then revealed his own contribution: another red. After careful sipping of the wine in all four bottles, the ambassador had to admit that Buchanan's was by far the best. Crawley and I thought so too. Léger was then chagrined to learn that Buchanan had in his car a whole case of this great wine — which he had bought in a shopping plaza in the suburbs of Paris. Rather a dour man, Buchanan barely ever smiled. But on the occasion of having trumped the ambassador with an inexpensive bottle of his own, he allowed himself a quick grin. (Crawley and I of course allowed ourselves rather more than that.)

Back in Canada, Roberge decided that he now had enough information to make a move and asked me to draft a memo to Jack Pickersgill, who as minister of Citizenship and Immigration reported to Parliament on the NFB. The first paragraph of the highly bureaucratic memo we signed on September 11, 1963, identifies its purpose: "to obtain a decision in principle on the support which could be forthcoming from the government of Canada for the development of a feature film industry."

The memo identified the condition of the Canadian film industry, with particular reference to entertainment films. It cited the fact that, although proceeds from film rentals in 1961 totalled $34.5 million, only $7 million of that was retained in Canada to pay salaries and the costs of maintaining theatres. It noted that in that same year three features were being produced in Canada, and that even a modest-sized entertainment film production industry in Canada could represent an additional $5 million a year. Moreover, a government investment would provide employment for a number of skilled filmmakers, writers, musicians, artists, actors, and technicians. The memo also stressed the importance of co-production agreements and pointed out that, as a result of the newly signed document with France, there was no question that the French film industry and Canadian producers could work effectively together. It proposed that the government immediately establish "a revolving development fund of $3 million set up for a three to four year period that would provide adequate assistance to launch a feature film industry in Canada."

It added that the government of Canada should take the lead in setting up a production funding system like the one in France, wherein a percentage of the national box office was pooled for French filmmakers, and further recommended that the governments of Ontario and Quebec levy a box office tax. In this way the provinces, "which collect amusement taxes at the box office, could be induced to return some part of this to Canadian feature film producers."

The last paragraph of the memo summed up the film commissioner's proposal:

> I am convinced that if we do not take action now, the opportunity to get a feature film industry in Canada may well be missed for another generation. There is a very great interest at the moment in feature films among writers, artists, and filmmakers across the country and among members of the film industry. But in this, as in many other fields, the inducements for talented individuals to realise their hopes outside the country are strong indeed. If the government could take decisive action I believe that by the Centennial year Canada would be occupying her proper place in the world of international cinema. May I say that I have greatly appreciated the interest you have always expressed on the occasions on which we have discussed this important matter.

The memorandum came back with a minute from Pickersgill applauding the idea and suggesting that an interdepartmental committee be set up to give it more study. We had finally convinced our minister that feature film deserved a support program of its own. Now we had to form a committee and win Cabinet approval. Suddenly, I had become the unofficial planner for the feature film industry.

CHAPTER 3
CULTURE VERSUS COMMERCE
1964–1965

The Montreal-based producer who first realised the business possibilities of making fearure films, especially for the Quebec market, was entrepreneur Pierre Lamy. The founder of Onyx, his producer credits include *Kamouraska* and *La Mort d'un Bucheron*.

T he official green light put pressure on us to set up the committee, and fast. In due course, it was dubbed "The Interdepartmental Committee on the Possible Development of a Feature Film Industry in Canada," an embarrassingly Canadian, doubt-stricken name. We weren't at all sure about winning approval, so Guy Roberge, who as usual knew all the players, proposed a committee that would be taken seriously by Cabinet.

To achieve an effective interdepartmental balance, we selected key representatives from the Department of Finance, the Department of Trade and Commerce, the Department of External Affairs (as it was then called), and the Secretary of State (which was responsible for the NFB). Roberge soon found officials at the mid-level of these departments who were sympathetic to the idea of a feature film industry. The committee was approved with Roberge as chairman, and the first meeting was held in January 1964 in the NFB's Ottawa office on Kent Street.

By this time I had done enough homework to discuss the activities of the National Film Finance Corporation in London and the Centre nationale de la cinématographie in Paris. I had also prepared research papers on the Australian recommendations for feature film industry support in that country and on the U.S. banks' lending policies, particularly the Bank of America, which was in those days Hollywood's main financial strong right arm.

At the committee's first meeting, Roberge referred to the first request on record for financial support for a Canadian feature film industry. It came from the AMPPLC, of which I had been an unofficial member for years. He named the titles of ten feature films either being produced or in the planning phase with total budgets of $4 million, the majority originating in Quebec. Also at the top of the agenda was Canada's newly signed co-production agreement

31

with France and a report on the discussions with the U.K. The committee members — all senior bureaucrats — were sceptical by nature, but Roberge managed to convey a sense of urgency and, after the first meeting, they agreed to meet once a week.

The committee invited two representatives of the Association professionelle des cinéastes to give their opinions: its president, Claude Jutra — whose first feature, a love story entitled *À tout prendre*, was already having a good run in theatres in Quebec — and Guy Côté, its secretary, who had made a study of government aid for feature films in Europe. They were very much in favour of the proposed fund.

The spellbinding Nat Taylor also made his pitch to the committee. A financially successful feature film industry, with income derived from foreign and Canadian sales, was perfectly feasible, he said. We met with other respected feature filmmakers, like Donald Haldane, who had directed *The Drylanders* in 1963 for the NFB. Everyone was in favour of the idea of a feature film fund.

At another meeting, Charlie Miller, the NFB's chief accountant, made a very positive financial forecast: "If the Government of Canada were to set up a $3 million fund for three years," he said, "the returns by way of interest, loans repaid, and profit participation would surpass $1 million by the end of the fifth year." In other words, an estimate of a $5 million return after five years on a first investment of $3 million was thought to be conservative. That wildly optimistic estimate was exactly what we wanted to hear, and at the time we had no reason to doubt it.

The committee soon began to see the line drawn in the sand between art and industry. To the question of "whether the effects of the proposed film industry should be economic — to help the balance of payments, stimulate employment, etc. — or cultural — to assist Canada's prestige abroad and to help biculturalism," the minutes record the committee response: "The industry should be primarily an economic operation with ancillary cultural effects." Films are, after all, both art and industry. Under the influence of Nat Taylor, the committee decided to tilt in the direction of industry.

We must have been thinking of the words of André Malraux, who, as Charles de Gaulle's famous minister of culture, said "Quoi qu'il en soit, le cinéma est par ailleurs une industrie." Regardless of whatever else it may be, cinema is an industry.

The committee reached a consensus, and in early May 1964 the Cabinet received its first report. By this time, Roberge's good friend, Maurice Lamontagne, had been appointed president of the Privy Council and secretary of state, so it was his job to look after our project and obtain Cabinet approval. Lamontagne, to our dismay, was not impressed with the report.

"It lacks substance," he said. He wasn't against the idea of federal funding for movies, but thought that a full-scale report on every aspect of the feature film business was necessary before the government could make an informed decision. The Cabinet accepted his recommendation to instruct the committee to produce a second, more detailed report. Roberge and I were upset at this delay, but begrudgingly set about preparing a new report.

In the meantime, the NFB's twenty-fifth anniversary celebration in 1964 provided a platform for the government to announce its intent to create a feature film fund. There was to be a special ceremony in its studio at which all the previous film commissioners would be present. As director of planning with no planning to do, I became the manager of this event and was to ensure that Canada's first film commissioner, John Grierson, was there. There was some doubt as to whether he would show up; he was having trouble with his drinking and wasn't in the best of health. I asked my old friend Sydney Newman, formely with the NFB and now a leading drama producer on British television, to attend and escort Grierson. On the day itself, I made Sydney promise that he and Grierson would arrive on time. They didn't. I was in a state of panic for over an hour. They finally showed up, perfectly sober, explaining that their taxi driver was geographically challenged.

Lamontagne's announcement about the government's intention to support Canadian feature film production with a separate Crown Corporation was well received by the press. As usual, however, the announcement had a divided response at the NFB: whereas the French producers were enthusiastic about the prospect, their English counterparts worried that the NFB might receive less support for documentaries and thereby lose its influence as the only advisor to the government on film matters.

Roberge was simultaneously forging ahead on the co-production front. We had signed a treaty with France and then had been politely rebuffed by the U.K. the same year. Undaunted, Roberge still hoped that the Italians could be persuaded to agree to a treaty. External had informed him of a telegram from Rome suggesting that this would be a good time for a meeting. Knowing that the successful signing of a treaty with Italy would be a valuable addition to our final report, we prepared for our trip to Rome with high hopes.

Pierre Juneau, director of French production at the NFB, had not only become a firm supporter of co-productions, but was actively engaged in putting together a four-part film about youth that involved Canada, France, Italy, and Japan. So Roberge decided to send both of us to Rome, with Juneau acting as chief negotiator while I would represent the interdepartmental committee.

Off we went. We couldn't believe our good fortune as we checked in to the legendary Grand Hotel on a brilliant sunny day before heading to the Canadian embassy. (Perhaps the blackbird singing near the goldfish pond in the embassy garden was a good omen?) Our confreres at the embassy had told us that, since the Italian legislation covering cinema wasn't due to be revised until the end of June, the Italians were unlikely to agree to a treaty with Canada before then. Nevertheless, Juneau, Pierre Charpentier of the embassy, and I sat down on the morning of April 10 in the high-ceilinged, grandiose boardroom of the Ministry of Foreign Affairs in the Foro Italico. Quite a contrast to our undecorated working spaces in Canada.

Across the table were Signors Cozzi, Orta, and Valignani, as well as their secretaries and assistants. Cozzi, who was from Foreign Affairs, was in favour of reaching an agreement. Orta, on the staff of the Ministry of Tourism and Spectacle, raised objections, however. He described the timing as "malheureux," and said that he thought his minister wouldn't be happy with an agreement that could result in Italian film technicians having less work in the future.

Valignani, secretary of the Italian Producers Association, pooh-poohed Orta's objections, claiming that a treaty would in fact result in *more* work for the Italian film industry. Despite their differences, we all agreed to review the existing Canada–France treaty clause by clause to arrive at the first draft of a new agreement. By the end of the day we had made significant progress and hurried back to the embassy to send Roberge a telegraphic update.

When we met a few days later with Valignani to go over the documents again, I was surprised to how intimately involved the secretary of the Producers Association was in their drafting. But it made sense, of course: the final treaty was for the benefit of the production industry, and who would know more about that than the producers themselves? The Association was even doing the typing and preparation of the documents, in English, French, and Italian, as part of its self-appointed role. The obviously close link between the Italian production industry and the nuts and bolts of government policy planning would have been unthinkable back home.

By the time of our final meeting, Valignani and I had become good friends. Short, a bit stout, and good-natured, he got the work done. By lunchtime we had witnessed the signatures of Charpentier and Cozzi on the documents. All that was needed now was the Italian Cabinet's approval — but that was months or even years away. I made a note in my diary: "Exactly why we got that telegram suggesting that this was a good time to sign an agreement may never be known." Thirty years later I wonder if Roberge's incomparable influence on the "old boy net" in External Affairs had been the reason. But how he did it remains a mystery.

In Rome one evening, I got a phone call from Peter Pearson, who was there studying. Having begun his career in Toronto at CBC Television, he had decided to learn filmmaking at an established film school. He wasn't impressed with the institutions in

New York, London, or Paris (there weren't any in Montreal or Toronto), so he enrolled at Il Centro Sperimentale's film school. Pearson invited me to the Centro, where we presented a program of Canadian films, and he came to the hotel on several occasions for meals and drinks at the ornate bar. I always picked up the tab, despite Pearson's not-too-insistent protests. He knew I was on an expense account. Many years later, when he became executive director of Telefilm Canada, Pearson was the one with the expense account.

During our time in the Eternal City I came to feel that Juneau had already decided that Quebec's film future lay in joint ventures with producers in France and Italy. He was uncomfortable running a production operation of prima donna filmmakers who, like Grierson's producers before them, were disinclined to listen to management. It wasn't long before Roberge realized that Juneau wasn't suited to that kind of management confrontation and told Judy LaMarsh, who by that time was the secretary of state, that Pierre was an ideal candidate to become the third member of the Board of Broadcast Governors. The Board had only recently been set up to regulate broadcasting, heretofore the exclusive domain of the CBC. Juneau's subsequent appointment would prove to be the real beginning of his distinguished career, one that eventually led him to become the first chairman of the CRTC and later chairman of the CBC. It is a record unlikely to be surpassed.

By this time, based on Judy LaMarsh's recommendation, Gordon Sheppard had become the secretary of the interdepartmental committee. I had been the first secretary of the committee and thought I was doing a good job; Roberge, though, wanted to avoid a confrontation with the minister and suggested that I could represent the NFB on the committee.

Famous in Canada for a CBC *cinéma-vérité* film about Lester Pearson, Gordon Sheppard had a hidden agenda, which became apparent only much later. When he persuaded LaMarsh that he could be a valuable addition to the committee, I doubt he mentioned that he wanted to produce a feature film with the support of the as-yet-to-be created agency. He certainly never told me at the time.

Meanwhile, rumours of a feature film loan fund had begun to circulate. The prospect spurred on the Quebec filmmakers, and several producers in Toronto and Vancouver also began to get projects underway. But all I could tell them was to "wait and see . . . the committee is at work." (As the Queen said to Alice, "Jam yesterday, jam tomorrow, but never jam today.")

The committee reconvened in October 1964 to consider what should be done about the Cabinet's decision instructing us to produce a second report. Two new powerful members had been added for this second go-round: J.F. Grandy of the Department of Finance and C.G.E. (Ernie) Steele from the Secretary of State, both of whom made important contributions. I remember Jim Grandy — with the swift stroke of a pen — changing $5 million to $10 million for the final report to Cabinet, and Steele skilfully shepherding the final legislation through all the red tape.

In phase two, we now had to contemplate how Canadian feature films were going to reach their audiences in Canada and abroad. Under the influence of Nat Taylor, Roberge and I had tended to brush that question aside in earlier committee meetings. Our single-minded idea had been to get some features produced — we'd face the distribution problems later.

Lamontagne disagreed. He thought that if he was to convince his colleagues in Cabinet, the distribution question had to be addressed. Conveniently, he had an associate on the staff of the University of Ottawa, Jack Firestone, who was also a professor of economics. Lamontagne dropped a hint to Roberge that Firestone would be an excellent consultant for the committee. In that era civil servants tended to be reluctant to hire any outside consultants, but Lamontagne was determined to have his man. Firestone was finally hired to study the distribution potential of Canadian cinema, and he set about completing an extremely detailed report.

To study the question of Canadian distribution, we had to turn to the owners of our cinemas — the U.S. majors. Taylor organized a meeting in New York with representatives from the studios, including the MPAA's Griffith Johnson, Robert O'Brian (MGM), Leo Jaffé (Columbia), and Charles Boasberg (Paramount). I was surprised to discover how vociferously they were against Canadian features. They clearly thought the Canadian proposal was a joke, and brought up all kinds of objections; I remember the meeting well. They simply could not — or would not — understand our enthusiasm for Canadian feature film production. Boasberg remarked that the prospect of such an activity "scared the hell out of me. It's difficult enough to make money with films made in the United States. What's the point of making them up there?"

In his patient way, however, Firestone kept bringing them down to earth. He insisted that he get some concrete recommendations to take back to the committee in Ottawa, and finally they came up with some ideas. Among them were the following:

 ◆ Make available studio and other technical facilities of the type that other foreign countries offer U.S. producers on attractive terms so as to make it possible for American firms to come to Canada rather than use their own facilities in Hollywood.

 ◆ Avoid discriminatory measures against American film producers and distributors, including screen and import quotas, special earmarked amusement taxes, taxation differentials, restrictions affecting the earnings of foreign film producers and distributors in Canada, artificial and non-economic regulations and barriers, "contents" requirements, etc.

The Americans appeared to compromise by suggesting that their own subsidiaries in Canada could send them scripts for consideration and act as intermediaries between Canadian producers and themselves. But we were asking for suggestions that would assist Canadian producers, and Canadian producers weren't even mentioned: the Americans' replies were strictly on their own behalf.

Firestone also raised the possibility that a deal could be worked out whereby 10 percent of U.S. earnings in Canada would be invested in Canadian production. But such a deal, the Americans said, would:

- represent discriminatory treatment of American film producers, who would be deprived of disposing of the 10 percent of their film earnings in Canada in the manner they considered to be in the best interest of their companies
- force the production of non-economic films in Canada, which would be neither in the long-term interests of Canadian film producers nor of participating American companies
- adversely affect the creativity and quality of films produced; Canada's international image would suffer if all that could be produced were mediocre feature films or motion pictures of even lesser quality, which are already being produced in large numbers all over the world and which in many instances lose money
- it would, if the conditions of Canadian government assistance included the requirement of employing a certain number of Canadian actors, technicians, and other production personnel, make it difficult for American producers to join in common ventures without being confident that Canadian stars, producers, and directors could have a similar public appeal as their American counterparts and that Canadian technicians and other production personnel were as competent as American staff available in large numbers to American major producers
- establish Canadian government interferences with U.S. private enterprise interests, which have hitherto operated without such interferences in Canada, and bring retaliatory action from the U.S. government affecting Canadian business in the United States.

It occurred to me that other countries had already faced such American threats, and that the Americans' attitude was designed to scare us off. But the prospect of retaliatory action was very real, as we would find out much later.

That was my first meeting with the majors as a group: it was a revelation. I liked them individually as they were all jovial fellows (on the surface). Underneath, however, they wouldn't budge an inch and I could sense a battle looming.

When it was finally completed in the spring of 1965, Firestone entitled his report "Film Distribution: Practices, Problems, and Prospects." Voluminous would be an understatement. Although he

39

had made it clear that we could expect opposition from the Americans, there was no way that Roberge was going to be dissuaded from getting a positive recommendation from Cabinet.

The committee hired other consultants, as well as asking John Terry, of the National Film Finance Corporation in England, and Jean-Claude Batz, an experienced civil servant from the cultural ministry in Brussels, to come to Canada to advise it. Meanwhile, Fernand Cadieux and I had each been working on reports on feature film production in Montreal and Toronto, respectively. Cadieux, who presented his report in April, was optimistic about producing feature films in the French language. When a member of the committee asked him why there was currently so much feature film activity in Montreal, he replied, "When a society becomes agitated as Quebec's society has, the people with dreams move quickly to try to realize those dreams." Cadieux's report recommended that the government provide 100 percent of the money for feature films, reasoning that "it was very difficult to prescribe that producers put up their own money when most of them had no money." He proposed "setting up a feature film industry by giving it a strong boost over a short period of time rather than spreading out the infusion of capital over a number of years." This idea did not attract the more conservative members of the committee.

My report was more down to earth than Fernand's. It would never have occurred to me to recommend 100 percent financing from the government. Instead I addressed more mundane subjects, including the importance of completion guarantees and the availability of technicians and technical facilities as well as financial and creative resources. "The desire of producers to make features certainly exists," I noted. "Their judgment of feature stories and their ability to inspire their crews and their casts to make films of high quality will have to wait the test of actual production." I hadn't the slightest idea, when I wrote that, that I might become involved in the process.

In May the committee gave final consideration to the Firestone report, which stipulated in no uncertain terms that a viable

Canadian film industry would have to get its films into theatres (and earn money with them) through American distributors and American-controlled theatres.

American features weren't as dominant as they are today, but even so, there was no doubt from the tenor of Firestone's report that the nascent Canadian film industry would have trouble getting into the U.S. market, where it would have to be if it was going to earn any money. Firestone speculated that, if a foreign-controlled chain had to find playing time for a Canadian film versus one provided by its own company, the American film would get priority and that the Canadian one would wait for a month, two months, six months . . . and in the meantime the producer wouldn't be getting any return on his investment.

Furthermore, he said, referring to the meeting with the MPAA representatives in New York, "Americans should not get government help to produce films in Canada on their own because they will come here solely for location work and not to co-produce." An inspired foresight.

Feature film legislation was listed as eighteenth in the C Category of the Legislative Priority List and would probably not get to the House of Commons before the fall. So the committee decided that the research phase had been completed, and delivered its second report to Cabinet in July 1965. It was accompanied by Firestone's report, as well as Cadieux's and mine. Under Roberge's dynamic chairmanship, the committee had managed to create about 500 pages of pertinent material. Once it had been carefully packed in boxes and carried up the stairs of the East Block, Michael Pitfield, a senior official in the Privy Council Office, looked at me and said, "You don't expect ministers to read all this stuff, do you?!" I replied, "Well, you asked for it!"

Ultimately, even the final report — at a mere ten pages — was too long for Cabinet, and our work was reduced to an executive summary that would be approved by Cabinet and form the basis of the legislation. Ironically, I could barely see the difference between this executive summary and the original memo to Jack Pickersgill that I had written for Roberge in 1963.

CULTURE VERSUS COMMERCE (1964–1965)

CHAPTER 4
THE CFDC RECEIVES ROYAL ASSENT
1966–1968

Photo : Lois Siegel.

When the late prolific author, Mordecai Richer (seen here in Montreal in 1972), heard about the creation of the CFDC, he wrote in the New Statesman: "The dizzying prospect of a Canadian film industry frightens me, when I dig into my own past experience of Toronto-based production companies."

J udy LaMarsh, the new secretary of state, was not very enthusiastic about the feature film industry. Yet when the House of Commons met on an afternoon in May 1966, LaMarsh was in her seat, ready to move that the House go into Committee to consider a resolution that $10 million be appropriated from the Consolidated Revenue Fund for the development of a feature film industry. This was a procedural step, which had to be taken before the legislation itself could be introduced. Up in the Gallery, Carl Lochnan from the secretary of state's staff and I were unloading our briefcases and getting ready to make notes on any points that the Opposition might bring up.

The minister knew we were up there, but it was a point of honour with her to handle the debate without having to wait for a message from us to be brought to her by one of the pages (and it would have been unthinkable for us to shout from the Gallery). There was a constant movement of pages across the green carpet between the pairs of seats assigned to the members of the House. In those days, pages were all men neatly dressed in black uniforms. The atmosphere was distinctly that of an English club, with hushed voices, except for the speakers. This was long before microphones and television cameras were allowed in the Chamber. The members of the Press Gallery, of course, were there to report on any questions that might embarrass the government. Since the Opposition set the pace at Question Time, and questions were the first order of business, we knew it might be some time before the House got to us.

Meanwhile, I could observe two old rivals. Seated beneath me was Prime Minister Lester B. Pearson, comfortably relaxed and chatting with other cabinet ministers. Opposition leader John Diefenbaker was busy gazing, hawk-like, at the government benches. I figured he was hoping to spot some weakness in the enemy's defence.

As the House worked its way through Question Period, the members and the journalists gradually dispersed until, late in the afternoon, only a few members and one or two pressmen were left. It was to this small audience that Judy LaMarsh was, at last, presenting the measure on which we had been working for the past three years.

LaMarsh began by referring to (but not apologizing for) the six-month delay since the public announcement of the government's intent to do something about Canadian feature films. She praised the previous minister, Maurice Lamontagne, but we knew that the impetus he had given to the idea of a Canadian feature film industry by supporting his good friend Guy Roberge, and most of the filmmakers in Quebec, had been reduced to zero by his resignation two or three months earlier. (Being rather politically naive, he hadn't seen any problem in making a deal to acquire some furniture on credit from a source that had contributed to his campaign. The subsequent row caused his resignation.)

As the debate on the resolution continued in the House of Commons, LaMarsh delivered a speech in June 1966 that Carl and I had worked on, which outlined all the arguments in support of a feature film industry in Canada. She then went on to warn Hollywood that we were serious:

> Many countries, in order to encourage the distribution of their own films, have applied quotas. We have chosen, however, not to introduce this kind of restriction in the bill at this time. Canadian films must, therefore, make it on their own merits. But in rejecting quotas we are counting on film distributors and cinema chains to give more than ordinary support to the aims of this program.

The minister was followed by the honourable member from Halifax, who was the spokesman for the Conservative opposition. Carl and I were relieved that he had decided to support the resolution. After all, the duty of the Opposition is to oppose. He even had a subject to recommend to the new Crown corporation once it was set up: Laura Secord, "that fine homespun heroine whose memory marches on in the pages of history books and on the covers of candy boxes." There was a bit of show business, I realized, in every member of Parliament. Although I had watched debates from the Public Galleries before, this was the first time I had a ringside seat. It was a fascinating experience to be so close to the speaker.

The spokesman for the NDP, Bob Prittie, also welcomed the legislation. He felt that the new Crown corporation would have some difficulty getting Canadian films distributed, and referred to the lack of ownership and control of Canadian movie theatres by Canadians. He had done his homework.

Prittie knew of *À tout prendre* and its director, Claude Jutra. He also hoped that directors Norman Jewison and Sydney Newman would soon return to Canada and start making features here. (They were both in the midst of successful careers, in Hollywood and London, respectively, with no intention at the time of returning to Canada.) He hoped Sidney Furie, a Toronto-born filmmaker who had just made his first feature on a shoestring, with financial backing from his relatives, would also be able to return to make his name in Canada.

As the debate continued, Howard Johnston, the member for Okanagan-Revelstoke, made a surprising statement. He had recently been in a movie house in London, England, he said, where "quite by accident I think," an NFB short, *Morning on the Lievre*, had been one of the films on the program. Being a Canadian, he was surprised and pleased when it received a spontaneous round of applause. From this small example, he optimistically forecast that if the quality of the films produced with the help of the proposed legislation would be as good as that, a flourishing industry, based in Canada, would surely be created.

"By adopting this legislation," he went on, "we will be putting a very small finger in a very large hole in the dyke through which we have been losing talent and money for a long period of time."

Next up was Ralph Cowan, the member for the York-Humber constituency in Toronto. He expressed the gravest doubts about the proposed legislation. Since the resolution was passed without a vote, we'll never know whether he would have voted for it or not, but he likely echoed what many MPs were thinking at the time: "This is terrific, absolutely terrific. We have so much money in the national treasury that we can throw $10 million into the development of a feature film loan fund. We can tell the aged and the infirm that we have not enough money to increase old age security pensions to $100 per month."

Apart from the political grandstanding, Cowan did raise one important point when he quoted a *Montreal Star* editorial: "The movie houses are tied tight to the big Hollywood companies. Will they be prepared to show Canadian-made films?"

Meanwhile, listening to a different drummer, a group of Quebec producers had a meeting in the Mount Royal Hotel in Montreal in April 1966, one month before Judy LaMarsh introduced the resolution in Ottawa. The meeting would lead to the founding of the Association des producteurs de films du Québec (APFQ), whose major role was to lobby governments, both provincial and federal. Among those present were directors Denys Arcand, Arthur Lamothe, Michel Brault, Gilles Carle, and the association's first president, Jean Dansereau. The meeting was largely concerned with "problemes d'ordres economiques, politique et moral qui interessent leur profession." These were mostly caused by Radio-Canada and the NFB, which weren't assigning enough production work to the private sector to keep their businesses going. Those present certainly knew about the proposed Canadian Film Development Corporation because some of them had been consulted by the interdepartmental committee. No doubt they were well aware of the snail's pace of bureaucracy, and they were right; it wasn't until January 1967 that the bill creating the CFDC was presented to the House of Commons, following the approval of the resolution.

On that day in 1967, Carl Lochnan and I were again in the Gallery ready to advise the minister on the legislation. By this time, however, David MacDonald, a United Church minister from Albaton and Tignish in Prince Edward Island, had been elected to Parliament as a Conservative. John Diefenbaker had assigned him the role of Opposition critic of the secretary of state's department, so it was he who was required to address the proposed Canadian Film Development Corporation Act.

MacDonald — a genuine movie buff — rose to speak. He made no bones about his disappointment that the government had seen fit to let this particular item languish on the order paper for so long; clearly a feature film industry in Canada was not a matter of terribly pressing concern to the government. The results, he said, were obvious: "We can leave the Chamber at this very moment and go down into the heart of the city where we can find half a dozen places where feature films are shown. I could even tell you the names of three or four of them. How come Canada does not have a feature film industry while even a small country like Korea has one?" Indeed.

Part of the answer, as MacDonald knew very well, and as Jack Firestone had told the interdepartmental committee, lay in the ownership and control of Canadian motion picture theatres. As an Opposition member MacDonald had a reason to point out the government's errors, and so he devoted part of his speech to the defunct Canadian Cooperation Project. He poured scorn on Prime Minister St. Laurent's government, describing how the Hollywood industry had duped it and how the MPAA had sold C.D. Howe on a weird scheme to promote travel by changing the dialogue of feature films to include the names of Canadian cities and tourist attractions.

MacDonald wound up his remarks:

> For thirty or forty years we have willingly exported millions of dollars of wealth to be entertained by motion pictures not produced in this country. It seems eminently sensible for us to take steps to ensure that some of the revenue gained from showing foreign films is put towards developing and encouraging a Canadian feature film industry. Now we should formulate the strongest legislation possible that will enable us to do this job.

THE CFDC RECEIVES ROYAL ASSENT (1966–1968)

Nat Taylor couldn't have said it better. Somehow, I thought, we *would* have a feature film industry, and it would eventually find its proper place in Canadian theatres.

During the course of the debate, the question of the NFB's influence on the work of the new Crown corporation came up. In the draft legislation before the House, the chairman of the proposed Canadian Film Development Corporation had no other responsibility than to chair the meetings. We, the bureaucrats, had not given the chairman a role in the day-to-day management of the Corporation. MacDonald had spotted this weakness. Up in the Gallery, still mesmerized with the excitement of watching our legislators at work, I realized that MacDonald was right. The lack of a strong CFDC chairman could put it at a disadvantage if a serious turf war broke out between it and the NFB.

LaMarsh had clearly understood what was going on. Nothing if not direct, she said in the House, "There is no suggestion — though I think from time to time this may have been raised — that the Film Board would attempt to strangle this industry to preserve itself." What better way of making sure that this wouldn't happen than by adding a full-time chairman, who could at least provide a counterbalance to the government film commissioner?

Fortunately, MacDonald pursued this idea of a full-time chairman to the point where the House took it seriously. Chagrined, since we hadn't thought of it ourselves in the interdepartmental committee, Lochnan and I indicated our approval from the Gallery by sending a note to the minister. After some further discussion, an amendment to create a full-time chairman of the CFDC was accepted. Paul Hellyer, the minister of National Defence, agreed to propose it after the chairman had ruled it in order. It's not very often that legislation is amended on the floor of the House.

The debate continued with John MacLean from Queen's, P.E.I., asking a pertinent question: "Won't some of this money be lost on unsuccessful films?" LaMarsh: "Without question we will lose some of this money, but it is our hope that we shall pick up more on the swings than we lose on the roundabouts — though that remains to be seen."

The future of the Canadian feature film industry would have to depend on English Canadians going to Canadian theatres in massive numbers to see Canadian-produced feature films. Our case was built on our optimism that this would happen. There was no concrete plan to regulate distribution, and theatres were a provincial responsibility. All that the new Corporation had to do was provide some of the money so that Canadian producers could accomplish miracles.

Having successfully introduced one amendment, MacDonald now tried to get the legislation changed to include a more precise definition of Canadian copyright ownership of the films that would be financially assisted by the new Corporation. At least 51 percent of the copyright should be owned by Canadians, he declared. The legislation stated only that it should be "beneficially owned" by Canadians. Unless this was clearly defined, he said, there would be a run on the funds by American producers seeking to make their own films with Canadian money. MacDonald was prepared to go down fighting:

> Then I, as an economic and cultural nationalist, will let it go on record at this point that I think the Minister has in this legislation opted for allowing a very sizeable chunk of what might have been a Canadian feature film industry to drift away from us. I hope that I do not have the opportunity at some future date of standing in this place and saying very loudly and clearly, "I told you so."

LaMarsh wouldn't budge. "Mr. Chairman, I would like to leave the wording as it is. My honourable friend is very young and I am sure that he has a hundred years left as a member of Parliament. Unlike myself, he will be here to make an assessment of the situation at some future date." MacDonald, who was born in 1936 and was therefore thirty-one at the time, was not only the youngest but also the most active participant in the debate. No doubt there was some feeling on the minister's part that he should be put in his place.

Finally we heard the magic words — "Is it agreed that the bill be read a third time, by leave, now?" — and LaMarsh moved the third reading. Our three years of planning, working, and dreaming were finally rubber-stamped when the Speaker subsequently said "Motion agreed to and bill read the third time and passed."

The legislation was speedily transferred to the Senate for the first reading in February. It was introduced by Jean-Paul Deschâtelets, whose long, detailed speech spanned several pages of the Senate Hansard and provided an excellent summary of the government's reasons for the legislation. Once again, no mention was made of the control Americans exercised over Canadian theatres. There was one short paragraph in French in which the senator pointed out that the bill had the support of Clement Perron, president of L'Association professionelle des cinéastes, and Jean Dansereau, one of its directors (the same Jean Dansereau who had recently become one of the founders of the APFQ). They were quoted as saying that although the bill did not go as far as they hoped, it had come at the right time and would lay strong foundations for a feature film industry in Canada.

The speaker for the Opposition was the formidable Senator Grattan O'Leary, a former editor of the conservative *Ottawa Journal*. "Honourable senators," he began, "I am sure we are all indebted to Senator Deschâtelets for his interesting and, I thought, beguiling explanation of this bill. This bill of course is a further adventure into state socialism. It is a further adventure in paternalism. It adds to the bureaucratic apparatus of the government."

O'Leary made by far the most eloquent speech on the bill's future:

> Senator Deschâtelets, at the conclusion of his speech, said that he saw no valid reason why this Corporation would not succeed. "There are many scores of valid reasons why this Corporation will not succeed, and I would hope that when the government is appointing a chairman it will appoint a good sound businessman and not leave the thing to be run by the go-go girls and the swinger boys of Toronto's Yorkville. . . . There is no sense in talking about our making films and selling them in Canada. We must have export markets. Therefore the films must have

extraordinary quality, and there must be extraordinary good business ability behind the enterprise to see that they are properly and sufficiently distributed."

I didn't attend the Senate debates, and I didn't know that Senator O'Leary would be the speaker for the Opposition. Had I known, I would certainly have asked to be present — this time in the Red Chamber — to hear an orator of the old school at the height of his powers.

When it came to the last stage of the parliamentary process, the creation of the CFDC was not considered to be sufficiently important to engage the attention of the Governor General. Fortunately, the Honourable John Robert Cartwright, Puisne Judge of the Supreme Court of Canada, was empowered "to do in His Excellency's name all acts on his part necessary to be done during His Excellency's pleasure." Thus did the CFDC Act receive royal assent and become the law of the land on March 10, 1967, in the presence of senators and members of the House of Commons. Despite the almost quixotic nature of the idea of creating a feature film industry, Guy Roberge and I had managed to get it taken seriously by the government.

The people of Canada had spoken: they clearly wanted a feature film industry of their own. But they weren't going to get it right away. True to her word, Judy LaMarsh continued to delay appointing a chairman and members of the Corporation. Between March and December 1967 she spent all her time being the minister responsible for the Centennial.

The year 1967 certainly was not a red-letter one for me. After Roberge left the NFB it had no work for me to do, but it nonetheless gave me office space and continued to pay for my secretary, Carole Langlois. We were like a ship without a rudder: the Corporation needed directors to function and the Canadian feature film industry seemed as far away as ever. I accepted a six-month contract from Pierre Juneau at the Board of Broadcast Governors, which paid for my trips to Ottawa during the week. There I was able to keep in touch with Ernie Steele, the undersecretary of state, hoping that he would remind the minister that, the Centennial notwithstanding, she ought to get on with making appointments for the CFDC.

In the early months of 1968 I received a call from Henry Hindley, who was working with Steele. He was a member of a small lunch club at Ottawa's Belle Claire Hotel where I had been a regular before the NFB moved me to Montreal in 1960. Hindley and I both understood the way things got done in Ottawa, and he had called to ask me to handle a diplomatic mission. He had sent me a letter, he said, signed by the minister, informing Georges-Émile Lapalme (the former leader of the Quebec Liberal party who subsequently became the first Quebec minister of culture) of his appointment as chairman of the Canadian Film Development Corporation. Since this would apparently be a potentially unpleasant surprise to Lapalme, Hindley suggested that I deliver it to him personally at his office in the Montreal City Hall, where he was a consultant to mayor Jean Drapeau.

Lapalme greeted me courteously, and when he opened the letter he expressed neither pleasure nor annoyance with the news. He asked who the other members of the Corporation were, and I listed George Elliot, Michèle Favreau, Royce Frith, George G.R. Harris, and Arthur Phillips — all selected by the Privy Council. I don't think he knew any of them, and I'm sure he was disappointed that he hadn't even received a phone call from the secretary of state herself. The letter also offered to make my services available to the Corporation in whatever capacity I could prove useful. Finally I was going to get a job in the Canadian feature film industry.

The first meeting was planned for April 1, or April Fool's Day. (Given the scepticism surrounding the new Crown Corporation, I suggested that it would be better on April 2.) With the exception of Harris, all the members of the Corporation were present at the first meeting in Ottawa; Ernie Steele came in the minister's stead. Only Favreau, who was at that time the film critic of *La Presse*, and Lapalme had French as their first language (indeed, I had been surprised that the Privy Council hadn't included more representation from Quebec), so most of the business was transacted in English. Favreau was also the only member of the Corporation who was not noticeably attached to the Liberal party. Frith, a Toronto lawyer with clients in the film industry, had served on the Royal Commission on Bilingualism and Biculturalism. (Frith and I, who shared an enthusiasm for bird watching, once set off in his Range Rover to look for birds in a marsh near his country place in Perth. Within a matter of minutes the wheels were spinning and the hubcaps were buried in mud — and our four-wheel-drive bird-watching adventure quickly turned into a four-footed slog to the nearest phone booth.) Arthur Phillips, the West Coast representative on the Board, was the mayor of Vancouver at the time. George Elliot was a senior officer of Maclaren's, the advertising agency in Toronto that I had previously run across in connection with the Canadian Cooperation Project.

Lapalme, who proved to be an excellent chairman, took the members of the Corporation through the bylaws, reading them out one by one and then looking around the table saying "Is it agreed?" Since the bylaws were mostly routine there wasn't much disagreement. Nor was there any disagreement with Lapalme's motion to make me the acting secretary of the Corporation. After the meeting we all had lunch at Cercle Universitaire and decided to hold our next meeting in Montreal.

According to the revision to the Act made when the legislation was in the House of Commons, Lapalme, as chairman, had a significant role to play. I took to meeting him in his house in Outremont, a large, comfortable redbrick not far from Pierre Elliott Trudeau's family house, as Lapalme pointed out to me on several occasions. It was here that he showed me the letter he had received from Prime Minister Pearson about his possible appointment as the Canadian ambassador in Paris. Reading between the lines, I realized that the letter was not a solid commitment, but I guess Lapalme wanted to believe that it was. But now I understood his feelings when I had presented him with Judy LaMarsh's letter.

55

Ambassador in Paris, after all, was light years away from being chairman of the CFDC.

At one of our meetings in his house, we discussed the question of where in Montreal the CFDC's headquarters should be located (there had never been any question that it should be in any other Canadian city). I had carried out a search of federal government buildings but couldn't find anything suitable in the downtown area where we wanted to locate. It would have eased our budget problem, because the $10 million allocated to the Corporation to make loans and investments and give grants and awards also had to cover our expenses. Finally, we decided that the best place would be Montreal's new Place Victoria, which had been completed just before Expo 67. The building was mostly black, with four white columns at each corner supporting its forty-odd storeys. The columns leaned imperceptibly inwards, giving an apparent conical shape to the building. No doubt the dramatic design was a factor in our decision to go to this particular building — after all, Lapalme had been the first minister of culture in any Canadian government. There was indeed a touch of grandeur in Georges-Émile Lapalme.

The Corporation had certainly created a lot of interest just by coming into existence as the first agency of its kind on the North American continent. It had even raised some eyebrows in England, where Mordecai Richler had been in residence for many years. In a January 1968 article in the *New Statesman* Richler raised a warning flag:

> The dizzying prospect of a Canadian film industry frightens me, when I dig into my own past experience of Toronto-based production companies. The archetypal Toronto film outfit has made indecently large profits out of TV commercials, or has perhaps produced a puerile but money-spinning series about Indians or Mounties and now set its sights higher — so to speak. They wish to make "a serious yet commercially viable film" with Canadian content.

Richler was being ironic, of course, but commercial viability was exactly what the new Corporation hoped to achieve. We were so happy with the successful creation of the agency that we overlooked the cautionary comments from Jack Firestone, who had warned us that the U.S. majors were not at all likely to cooperate.

THE CFDC RECEIVES ROYAL ASSENT (1966–1968)

CHAPTER 5
"YES, BUT . . ."
(1968–1970)

Seen here on the set of *The Act of the Heart*, Canadian star Donald Sutherland chats with cultural bureaucrat Michael Spencer who loved getting out of the office.

"Cultural bureaucrat" was a term that didn't exist in 1968. But if the Canadian Film Development Corporation didn't invent the designation, its staff was certainly the first to exercise the function. We were a new breed of civil servant, born from the need for government involvement in creative and artistic ventures. The industry assumed we had only to open the doors and say: "Here's the money." But I knew it wasn't going to be as easy as that.

This was the dilemma: the Federal Industrial Development Bank lent money to business enterprises and the Canada Council gave grants to artists, including some filmmakers. Now, as a cultural agency using commercial criteria, or vice versa, we had to find our place somewhere between these two poles. That culture–commerce hybrid has caused confusion since day one.

Georges-Émile Lapalme was a good choice as CFDC chairman. He was lucky to be supported by the new prime minister, Pierre Elliott Trudeau, and his secretary of state, Gérard Pelletier, who were both keen on cinema. In fact, Pelletier's wife, Alex, was a scriptwriter.

The political stage was set and the money was in place; what we needed now was a model. Fortunately, I had spent several years finding out how government film agencies worked in other countries, and this information would serve us in good stead as we faced an impatient industry that had waited five years for this moment. The applicants were clamouring for money to flow in their direction.

We had invited John Terry, executive director of the National Film Finance Corporation (NFFC) in London, England, to meet the interdepartmental committee at the planning stage in 1965, and we subsequently invited him to come to Montreal. Terry explained to us that in the U.K. it was the directors of the NFFC who

61

decided which films would be supported. (I don't remember the backgrounds of those directors, but I'm sure that none of them came from the film industry.) Terry had a puckish sense of humour. "If the papers on which their decisions were based were left on the table overnight and the charwomen read them," he laughed, "their decisions would be just as good as the directors.'" He knew better than anyone that chance plays a big role in show business.

Terry also made it clear that the NFFC would never approve a project if it wasn't accompanied by an agreement from an established company to distribute the picture after it was completed. The logic of this argument was persuasive, so at our second meeting we decided to follow the U.K. precedent. We too insisted that the producer had to have a distribution deal. Since, as chairman and secretary, Lapalme and I had full powers to co-sign contracts, we reviewed each file with the members and determined how much support each project should be given.

I decided on a formula that might be characterized by the phrase "Yes, but . . . ." The "buts" included: "Your script is okay, but your production people don't have enough experience;" or ". . . but you can't use American writers;" or ". . . but you don't have a distributor." These responses took the edge off a direct refusal. And even if I felt the answer should be no, I always added a challenging "but". This, of course, made sure the project would come back to a subsequent meeting. In some cases we were at the beginning of a lengthy bargaining process, one that I would eventually find to be the most rewarding part of my role of cultural bureaucrat.

The other significant hurdle for the applicants was where to get the rest of the money. The committee had assumed right from the beginning that CFDC funds would be only a part of the financial package. The Corporation was there to help the private sector produce feature films, but it also had to make the money go as far as it could and to make sure the producers would pony up their share. That's why we decided at the outset to limit our contributions to 50 percent of the budget (or less) with a maximum of $200,000.

In 1968 Quebec producers were out in front; they had the best-developed projects. Cinépix (John Dunning and André Link) already had *Valérie*, Denis Héroux's love story about a prostitute with a heart of gold, in the theatres. Onyx (Pierre Lamy with his brother André) had just acquired Niagara, a small, well-equipped Montreal studio that had an ongoing contract with the CBC. "When the Lamy brothers took over the company," Dunning told me, "they made a deal with the CBC to complete all the shows that Niagara had under contract." But Onyx's real objective was to get a studio and its equipment so that it could make movies on studio downtime, namely on the weekends.

Before the CFDC had even had its second meeting, I visited the set of *Le viol d'une jeune fille douce* — a crazy road movie about three brothers pursuing the man they think is responsible for their sister's pregnancy — and watched its writer, Gilles Carle, direct a scene. Actor Donald Pilon was there, and recalls the excitement of beginning his acting career with Carle's no-budget, improvisational style: "I don't know how many weekends it lasted, but I know we got about five hundred bucks for the whole thing!" His experience was typical of many Quebec movies being made at the time. Their multi-tasking often turned the cast into crew: "On the weekend, Pierre Lamy would bring the equipment and we were the crew. There was a sound guy. There was a cameraman. There was the director, and that was all. We had to move the cameras and what-not. So we didn't help the crew; we did it ourselves."

Pilon also chuckled at the idea of a written dialogue:

> There was no script — I'd tape a few notes on the dash of the car and the cameraman would fix the camera on the car for us. We couldn't have him or the soundman with us. In the car there were only four of us: my brother, Daniel; this other fellow (whom I can't remember the name of); and the girl sitting between Daniel and myself. And they had told us that what's expensive in a film is the film, so Gilles would say: "Drive on for about three or four minutes," and with my notes, we'd make up the dialogue. That's what we'd do! And when we'd think we were "about there," I'd jump out of that car and I'd stop that camera as quick as I could.

The energy was contagious. Even Larry Kent (who had come from Vancouver to shoot a feature in Montreal) and director Claude Jutra volunteered to sacrifice their weekends to act in the film.

The savvy Lamy brothers, well aware of the Quebec box office success of Carle's *La vie heureuse de Léopold Z.*, soon made a deal to provide equipment and a crew for *Le viol*. Pierre Lamy and I had been friends for years, and he was wise enough to keep me up to date with what was going on at Onyx. In return, I kept him abreast of our proposed plans for rules and regulations, most notably that we would expect the producers and distributors to provide some of the money.

Lamy had definite plans to become an important producer of feature films, and swiftly persuaded brothers Denis and Claude Héroux, as well as Claude Fournier and Marie-José Raymond, to join Onyx. They all wanted to make features, and I'm sure Lamy must have told them that he had a good contact at the CFDC. As soon as *Le viol* was finished shooting, Lamy got Carle started on the script of *Red*, a crime thriller starring Daniel Pilon as a Métis used car salesman accused of murder. Meanwhile, Fournier and Raymond were writing *Deux femmes en or*, a delightful romp about two suburban housewives who, frustrated by their husbands' absence, find solace in the arms of assorted handymen. The film would become the most popular feature ever produced in Quebec. Onyx, one of the first producers out of the gate to apply to the CFDC, was on a roll.

Other important proposals arrived at the new Place Victoria CFDC headquarters. One of them was Paul Almond's *The Act of the Heart*, a dramatic story of a woman struggling with her religious convictions. Almond, who had been a television producer and director for the CBC for many years, had already written his first feature film, *Isabel*, about the trials of a young girl from Montreal returning to the Gaspé after her mother's death. He had discovered Geneviève Bujold in Montreal, and after starring her in several of his CBC productions, went on to cast her as the lead in *Isabel*. He also managed to get a major U.S. studio, Paramount, to finance the picture. And, given that *Isabel* was in distribution by the time the CFDC opened its doors, Almond had already met two conditions for CFDC support: a previous film in distribution and an offer to invest from a distributor.

The proposal was delivered to my office by messenger and, a day or two later, the buzzer in my apartment on Nun's Island announced the unexpected arrival of Almond and Don Johnston. "We're here on a matter of great urgency," Almond said, and introduced me to Johnston: "He's my lawyer on the picture." "What picture?" I asked, playing for time. "*The Act of the Heart*, of course. I've got Geneviève Bujold and Donald Sutherland lined up. Universal will distribute. We need $200,000 to cover 50 percent of the budget."

I couldn't believe these guys had just appeared on my doorstep. "Perhaps we can deal with this in the office?" I countered. "No way," Almond said. "You don't understand show business. Universal wants to know if you're in. Now. It's only four p.m. in L.A." Although I had the excuse that investment decisions were made by the Board, I felt defensive about it. How would Sam Goldwyn or Darryl Zanuck react? I wondered. They'd come down on the side of the producers, of course! So the next morning I called the Board members, who were pleased to be consulted so urgently and who agreed with the decision to invest. It was easy for me to be convincing with Universal in the mix.

Donald Sutherland was to play the role of a troubled priest in the film. Born in New Brunswick, he had begun his career in Europe and by this time had begun to establish himself in Hollywood. Sutherland, like so many other Canadian-born performers, from Fay Wray to Jim Carrey, had gone where the challenge would be the greatest, and had already got his first break appearing in *The Dirty Dozen* in 1967. The first time I had the pleasure of meeting him was when *The Act of the Heart* was on location at Saint Joseph's Oratory in Montreal. Shortly after this his

"YES, BUT . . . ," (1968-1970)

65

career took off with Robert Altman's smash hit *M*A*S*H*. From there he never looked back. One of the most prolific actors in the industry, in 1970 alone he appeared in five films (*The Act of the Heart, Start the Revolution, M*A*S*H*, Kelly's Heroes, Alex in Wonderland*). But despite his international success, Sutherland has always kept a foot in Canada.

Indeed, meeting such talent proved to be one of the perks of being CFDC boss, and I never missed an opportunity to go on set. Although standing around waiting for the next take can be dull, the ambiance is exciting (and I was always looking for an excuse to get out of the office). The shooting of *The Act of the Heart* also generated a lot of excitement in the media. Even *Time* magazine used a shot of Bujold on its cover that week (Canadian edition only, of course). The film raised our spirits in the CFDC — we were sure we were doing the right thing to launch our infant industry.

We'd been able to establish a fifty–fifty financing structure with Universal for the film; the CFDC was pleased and so were they. Had I been more experienced, though, I would have known that Universal had agreed to the deal only because they thought Bujold was about to become a major star (two years later, in 1970, she was nominated for an Academy Award) and they wanted her to sign a long-term contract.

That was probably why our negotiations in Los Angeles went so well. The CFDC had, as yet, no staff lawyer, so I hired a friend of Lapalme's, Réal Bisonnette, to negotiate for us. He had no show business experience, but he carefully read all the fine print and made suggestions for changes, which were accepted by Universal's lawyers. We were insisting on getting our share of the profits, believing that Almond's script and brilliant performances by Bujold and Sutherland would translate into some return on our investment. What we didn't realize was that Universal would control the advertising expenditures and the release schedule to suit themselves. On the other hand, we had a Canadian film in release by one of the major Hollywood studios. And there I was, signing contracts

"YES, BUT . . . ," (1968-1970)

on the antique French desks and tables (a tax write-off) that Universal used to furnish its office in Burbank.

The euphoria of those early days was intense. I kept having to remind myself that I wasn't really a movie mogul, even though I was sitting on a $10 million dollar federal government fund with dreams of creating a profitable feature film industry in Canada. The idea seemed perfectly feasible. *Valérie* was on its way to its first million dollars in ticket sales. It helped that the new executive director at the Quebec Board of Censors, André Guerin, had allowed producers to show more than a hint of breast and thigh in the lovemaking scenes.

Cinépix, which had handled the distribution for *Valérie*, soon had a couple of projects of its own on the table. Concealed under coy working titles *The Looking Glass* and *V . . . pour Victoire*, we approved them without a detailed review of the content. After all, they had come from reputable producers, although we did include a clause in the investment contract stating that the producers would make any cuts required by the provincial censor boards. (Dunning and Link invited me on the sets, of course, but for official visits they chose innocuous scenes; for example, when Danielle Ouimet was wearing business attire in an office setting.)

The Act of the Heart and Jean-Pierre Lefebvre's *La chambre blanche* were the first two features that the Corporation financed. The contrast between them is startling: *The Act of the Heart* hoped for an audience of millions; *La chambre blanche* was a small *film d'auteur*, a poetic vision of episodes in the life of a couple. One was in English, the other in French. One had a budget of $500,000; the other $90,000. *The Act* was shot in colour; *La chambre* in 35 mm black and white. Since our aim was to bring a feature film industry into existence, we thought both projects were eligible. It was our view that the industry couldn't survive unless we supported a wide variety of Canadian movies.

In the first couple of years, the Corporation never wavered from the belief that its investments in Canadian features would form the basis of a flourishing film industry. But it had a political duty as well. It was owned by the people of Canada and, as trustees, the Corporation had to decide at every meeting whether the proposal before us would make money, be popular with Canadian audiences, or both. (Or neither.) We were hopefully fulfilling our mandate both commercially and culturally.

By then, I had an experienced budget controller on staff, Ronald "Pete" Legault, to assure me that production budgets were legitimate. We kept an eye on the producers and the shoot itself. In those days my main apprehension was that the film wouldn't be delivered at all and that the money would be lost. On the other hand, the desire to make the movies and get them in front of audiences was so motivating that I sometimes felt guilty about letting producers get into more debt than they could handle. In the end, I decided that it was their responsibility, not mine. (Guilt is one of the hazards of being a cultural bureaucrat; a hazard I tried very hard to avoid.)

Meanwhile, Corporation members had been given a copy of Jack Firestone's voluminous report on distribution that underlined the opposition of the U.S. majors to an independent Canadian industry. We were sure the English-language Canadian distributors had also read the report, but we knew we had to have their cooperation if we were to succeed in getting producers, writers, and directors in Canada to make features for the world market. For that, we would need a functioning industry, meaning both production and distribution.

To that end, Lapalme and I met the members of the Canadian Motion Picture Distributors Association. The meeting, unfortunately, provided only "a useful exchange of views," to quote the Corporation's minutes. It wasn't until a year later that we realized this was a euphemism for stonewalling. No doubt the MPAA had something to do with it. After all, Canadian distributors depended on MPAA members for 90 percent of the films they needed for their normal business; no wonder they'd resist financial involvement in projects from English-language producers.

It was at this stage that I got to know George Destounis of Famous Players, the major theatre chain in Canada. Pierre Lamy had asked him for an investment in *Red*, Gilles Carle's next film after *Le viol d'une jeune fille douce*. Of Greek descent, Destounis was born in Montreal; he had started in the movie business as an usher and worked his way up to president. John Sperdakos, Famous Players' director of public relations at the time, remembers him as a man of great determination and administrative talent. Destounis's knack for mathematics was legendary, retaining as he did all the weekly box office figures of more than 100 theatres in his head. Perhaps because he hadn't been born in the U.S., he had no preconceived opinions about the superiority of the American feature films.

Destounis believed that the CFDC could make a significant contribution to the Canadian production scene and was ready to come up with his share. When I went to see him for the first time, in Ottawa's Chateau Laurier Hotel, I found him lying on his bed reading a newspaper. "Pierre Lamy suggested this meeting, Mr. Destounis," I said. "You've already invested in *Red*. If Famous is going to keep on putting money into Canadian films, I have a suggestion: *À soir on fait peur au monde*." The film had all the earmarks of a box office hit. It was a live concert film starring Robert Charlebois, who at the time was as popular in Quebec as Céline Dion is today. Destounis was immediately interested, getting off the bed and strolling around the room in his waistcoat. Well over six feet tall and heavily built, he was a man who liked to get directly to the point. I explained that there were other producers in Quebec he should know about and that the role of the CFDC was to get the industry rolling. It wasn't really my job to do the sales pitch, but we got on well enough to have a handshake deal to finance the film. Only then did we inform the producer, Jean Dansereau, and his director, François Brault, that a fifty–fifty financing deal was sealed. Once again, as in the case of *The Act of the Heart*, I somehow ended up in the role of executive producer, an acting secretary sandwiched somewhere between the government and private enterprise.

A year later, in 1970, the box office revealed that the public wasn't impressed with *À soir on fait peur au monde*, despite all the positive reviews (and there had been many, in both the French and English press) and the presence in the cast of such Quebec icons as Gilles Vigneault (who was also in *The Act of the Heart*), Louise Forrestier, and Jean-Pierre Ferland. The producers hadn't transferred to the screen the enthusiasm Robert Charlebois brought to his live performances, and the movie proved a pale shadow of the stage shows.

With French-language production thriving in Quebec, the CFDC reasoned that Toronto should be the creative centre of English-language production in Canada, and looked for proposals that had box office potential to galvanize the production scene there. Thus was *Flick* given the go-ahead. Toronto producers Bill Marshall and Gil Taylor had submitted the script — a far-out Frankenstein story involving brain manipulation set on a Toronto campus — and had found the requisite distribution deal and 50 percent financing from the private sector. Even though Marshall and Taylor's track record was strong only in TV commercials and industrial production, we approved the picture. It was shot quickly and was in the theatres eight months later. The reviews, alas, were dreadful. Martin Knelman's *Globe and Mail* review was headlined "*Flick* Is a Horror, All Right: All Canadian, All Lousy." ·

Gil Taylor, who has since had a very successful career in the film industry, defends *Flick* for what it was:

> Bill and I said right from the start: "Well, let's make a B movie." And that's exactly what we did. And actually for that genre, it was a good B movie. But when it came out, then everybody said, "Oh my God: they've made a B movie." And we said: "Yeah, and that's what we told you we were going to do. We were doing a Roger Corman type of deal." As a matter of fact, Roger Corman said it was as good as anything he'd done. Yet Canada didn't understand at the time that there was a place for B movies.

It was the first time the role of the Corporation had been denounced in the media. The Montreal press had never questioned the role of government in the entertainment industry, but in the *Globe*, Knelman was scathing about the Corporation's efforts to date: "A couple of crummy movies are no great crime, especially since the CFDC is bound to make its money back. But it would be a bad joke if making its money back was all the CFDC aspired to." (As a matter of fact, we never did recover our investment in *Flick*.) At its next meeting the Corporation decided not to reply to press criticism of the films it invested in, leaving that responsibility to the producers. The critics, we determined, wouldn't sidetrack the quest for a viable film industry in Canada, even though their barbs were often hard to take.

In *The Toronto Star*, then-entertainment reporter Sid Adilman took a different tack. He wrote a piece that compared *Flick* and *Stereo*, horror director David Cronenberg's first film, simply on the basis that two different kinds of filmmakers had "won special consideration" from the CFDC. Adilman noted that Cronenberg's two films to date — *Stereo* and *Crimes of the Future* — had reached merely tiny, specialized audiences, which "proves that the CFDC isn't only concerned with the mass commercial market type of movie." He hit the nail on the head: the Corporation obviously planned to invest in features ranging from *films d'auteur* (*La chambre blanche* or *Stereo*) to pop culture (*Flick*).

Two other Toronto-based productions turned out to be major disappointments. The first of these was 1969's *Explosion*, produced by Julian Roffman and Nat Taylor and directed by Jules Bricken. It was a measure of Taylor's confidence in this project that he had asked the Corporation for a loan, believing that the picture would be successful enough at the box office to pay us back. He had personally chosen Bricken and his script, even though Bricken wasn't a Canadian and hadn't had much experience in making feature films. Taylor was overwhelmingly persuasive, however, and I relied on his judgment. He had aspired to become the Sam Goldwyn of Toronto, but producing profitable features, it turned out, was not his forte.

One year later, the Corporation knew the picture wasn't going to make any money; Taylor had asked us to change the loan to an investment so that he wouldn't have to pay us back. Up to that point I had been convinced that the CFDC could be profitable. Now I was beginning to wonder if the quest for a feature film industry in Canada would be successful after all. And, more to the point, could it make money?

The CFDC had also invested in other Toronto-based features, such as *A Married Couple*, director Allan King's follow-up to his 1967 production *Warrendale*, a *cinéma-vérité* study of a home for disturbed children that had been originally produced by the CBC and distributed in theatres by Columbia Pictures. *Warrendale's* real situations and the authentic nature of its dialogue had excited audiences. *A Married Couple* — an intimate portrait of a deteriorating marriage — did not arouse the same enthusiasm.

The Corporation was discovering what the international industry had known all along: that it was difficult to tell from a script what would turn out to be a commercially successful film. But that's show business.

Nonetheless, all this action in Toronto encouraged us to sign a lease for an inexpensive office in a shopping mall on Bloor Street, a move that would clearly distinguish us from all the other government agencies in office buildings. We had initially thought we needed an office only in Montreal, but we soon found out that Canada is a nation of fiercely competitive principalities. Quebec had the headquarters of the CFDC, so there had to be an office in Toronto.

Vancouver wasn't yet a part of that competition, despite the success of local filmmaker Larry Kent, who before moving east had produced two low-budget films (*The Bitter Ash* and *Sweet Substitute*) during his student days at the University of British Columbia. Nonetheless, we flew to Vancouver for meetings with putative feature film producers and a group that was planning to build a film studio in the suburbs.

By chance, director Robert Altman was shooting *That Cold Day in the Park* in Vancouver. He had planned to shoot in London, where there's plenty of rain, but changed his mind when he met Canadian location manager Jim Margellos in Los Angeles. Margellos told him that it rains just as much in Vancouver, where the shoot would be cheaper and more convenient. Margellos got the job.

Altman accepted the invitation to meet the members of the Corporation. Like all good directors he was also a good communicator, and we were fascinated by the story he told of raising money for this, his first feature as an independent producer/director. He really wanted to break out of the studio mould, which was exactly what we wanted Canadian producers to do. And as his future career made clear, directing *M*A*S*H* was only a stepping stone. His good experience in Vancouver led him to shoot another film there, *McCabe and Mrs. Miller*. In later years Altman shot several more features in Canada, becoming the first American director to find and use our technical talent and creative resources.

The same trip resulted in another surprise encounter, this time with Guy Côté, a former colleague from the NFB who had come to the meeting at Lapalme's request. While I'd been running the Corporation as acting secretary the search for an executive director had continued, and after interviewing several candidates the members had narrowed down their choice to Côté and myself. They expected to make a final decision at the Vancouver meeting.

Côté was still on the staff of the NFB. He had worked in both its distribution and production branches, especially in the London office. There he had used his spare time to good effect, amassing an important library of books on film that he continued to collect until he donated them to the Cinémathèque Québécoise. CFDC members didn't want to appear to have overlooked Quebec, and felt that Côté was the best Quebec-born candidate. They made a good political decision and recommended both of us: Côté as executive director and myself as secretary.

Secretary of State Gérard Pelletier was perplexed by the rec-ommendation. He apparently thought that I should be executive director, and asked if we could meet at his office in the Parliament Buildings to discuss the matter. Pelletier was close to the Quebec industry, and knew that I had its full support to become executive director. The truth is that I really wanted the job, but I was too polite to ask for it. And on Côté's part, it was a question of pride. He would probably refuse to work under me, whereas I would (even if slightly begrudgingly) work under him. Pelletier had called this meeting with me to insist that I convince the members to change their recommendation and nominate me for the position. Quite an assignment, but I succeeded.

In November 1969 Pelletier named Quebec playwright and actor Gratien Gélinas as the new CFDC chairman. In 1952 Gélinas had starred as a Chaplinesque soldier in the Canadian army in the famous Quebec feature *Tit-coq*. Best known for his stage character Fridolin, he was a household name in the Quebec entertainment industry and was also well known in English Canada; he gave the CFDC some status. I looked forward to working with him. As chairman and executive director, we would together take the CFDC further toward its goal of creating a Canadian feature film industry.

"YES, BUT . . . ," (1968-1970)

CHAPTER 6
THE CFDC GETS ROLLING
1971–1972

Photo : Lois Siegel.

Paul Almond, director/producer/screenwriter of *The Act of the Heart* celebrates at the Ritz during the Montreal World Film Festival.

Gratien Gélinas quickly became known as a hands-on chairman. He knew show business, and in his view, reading scripts and telling producers how they could improve their stories was part of his role as a leader. He wasn't Quebec's premier playwright for nothing.

It was Gélinas's rejection of a proposal that led to an early lesson in the downside of being executive director. In 1971 Cinépix talked to me about their plans for a feature film entitled *Le diable est parmi nous*. Since John Dunning and André Link's track record had been impeccable, I let them know that CFDC approval could be taken for granted. I spoke too quickly! Three weeks later, when the proposal arrived, Gélinas was unimpressed. He thought we should refuse it.

Michèle Favreau, the only other French-speaking person on our Board, supported Gélinas, and the other members soon followed. That left me with the embarrassing task of informing Dunning and Link that the CFDC wouldn't approve the project. Oddly, for once, their instinct for what the public wanted failed them: when *Le diable* was released in 1972, it was a near disaster in the theatres.

Gélinas was right that time, but he found it a lot more difficult to deal with Gilles Carle. As the executive director, I had recommended to the Corporation that we invest in *Les mâles*, his follow-up film to *Red*. Gélinas read the script and of course wanted to suggest improvements. I knew they wouldn't be well received by the producers, and so to discuss the matter we met with Carle and Pierre Lamy at Gélinas's summer cottage at Oka. The meeting ended in a shouting match between Gélinas and Carle, with Lamy and I sitting bemused on the sidelines. Not surprisingly, Carle, who was extremely stubborn, came out of the discussions without a single line changed.

He had my full support. I had gone to one of the downtown theatres on Ste. Catherine Street where one of his films was playing, and the audience's response told me that he knew very well what the Quebec public would pay to see. I can imagine how much he must have enjoyed sitting in the theatre and hearing the crowd around him laugh at his jokes. And while he wouldn't take any criticism from Pierre Lamy or anyone else in the cutting room during production, I noticed that after a premiere he wasn't opposed to the idea of taking the film back for further editing if he got the impression from the audience that it wasn't working. He was a pioneer of test marketing.

By the early 1970s, the second wave of Quebec features was in its theatres. *Red* achieved a box office return of $200,000 in no time. *V . . . pour Victoire* and *The Looking Glass* (now retitled *L'initiation* and *Love in a Four Letter World*, respectively) swiftly followed. These pictures were all running in Famous Players theatres, so if George Destounis had lost money on the Robert Charlebois picture, he was certainly making it on these two films, in Quebec and elsewhere across the country.

John Dunning and André Link had already established their reputation in 1969 with *Valérie*. Its star, Danielle Ouimet, had been making personal appearances in theatres across Canada and causing quite a stir because of her controversial nude scenes. "Women would protest and picket the theatres carrying signs that said 'She's the Devil.' They thought I wouldn't show up, but I did," Ouimet told us. Owing to the opposition of its censorship board, Ontario was the last province to accept the film.

Despite the setback of *Explosion*, we continued to trust Nat Taylor's judgment. He had strongly recommended the appointment of Wolfe Cohen, a Canadian senior executive from Warner Bros., as the CFDC's man in New York. Since we were still thinking that working with the Americans was the best way to advance the Canadian feature film industry, we agreed and signed Cohen to a two-year contract for 1970 and 1971. His job was to propose Canadian scripts and projects to his numerous contacts in the business, underlining that the Canadian government expected him to increase the number of Canadian features in American and Canadian distribution. He would be our man on the spot.

Cohen, a Canadian citizen, had no intention of leaving New York, which had been his home for many years. He knew a lot of people in the business, and certainly worked hard looking for American distributors. As I discovered on one of my trips to work with Cohen, most of them were a bit eccentric (one even had a barber's chair behind his desk). After dismissing our proposals they would invariably ask us to read the backlog of scripts in their files that could be "Canadianized" with a few minor changes and put into production with our money. Optimistically, we had hoped Wolfe would get a few more productions like *The Act of the Heart* going. But that wasn't really a good calling card; it hadn't done much business. At the end of the day, American distributors just didn't want what we had to offer.

The Americans had absolutely no reason to work with the Canadian industry, except that they could use the money. To get it, American producers sent scripts directly to us in Montreal, and I spent too many hours on the phone discussing them. I wasn't hard-nosed enough — perhaps I was too polite. The scripts they wanted us to co-produce had no Canadian content. Who needed it? Nothing had changed since the Canadian Cooperation Project. Cohen did succeed in getting Canadian scripts into the hands of the readers employed by U.S. producers and distributors, but that's all. It was a dialogue of the deaf.

There were exceptions. Lester Persky and Lewis Allan — American producers who were aware of Canada's emerging interest in creating a feature film industry — had persuaded MGM to take an interest in the Canadian play *Fortune and Men's Eyes*. While I thought there might be a problem about showing sexual activity between men (in prison or elsewhere) on screen, there was no doubt that the play could be turned into a significant motion picture. By coincidence, at one of our first CFDC meetings we had received a proposal for the same play from Donald Ginsberg of Toronto's Elgin Films, and so he became the co-producer with Persky and Allen. We had invested $25,000 in pre-production at the end of 1968.

In those days, Canadian content was determined by the members of the Corporation under Section 10 of the CFDC Act. They would decide if the film had significant Canadian creative, artistic, and technical content. The picture certainly qualified, since Ginsberg was also its editor, while most of the cast, crew, and technical support came from Toronto. I even had the chance to indulge my growing interest in visiting sets by making a trip to the Quebec City location, an abandoned jail close to the Plains of Abraham.

Harvey Hart, the director, was working from a script by John Herbert, the original playwright. Hart was a Canadian who had worked with Sydney Newman in the U.K. and in Toronto as a television director. We insisted on Hart, though Persky and Allen were pushing heavily for an American, Jules Schwerin. The film starred Wendell Burton and was subsequently released in the U.S. market to very good reviews.

Even though American distribution companies were involved, there was no doubt in my mind that *Fortune and Men's Eyes* and *The Act of the Heart* were Canadian feature films in the real sense of the word. I hoped that the emerging industry would produce many more like them — Canadian stories that would attract the mass audience. The challenge, of course, was that English Canadian audiences had been long conditioned to the American style of entertainment in movie theatres.

By this time we knew that if we were to succeed in English-language production we would have to work with the industry in Toronto, where our small staff —Chalmers Adams and Lillian Gauci Brooks — were beginning to discuss projects in earnest with prospective directors and producers. One of the projects the CFDC invested in during this time was Don Shebib's first feature, *Goin' Down the Road*, although it was initially the CBC's Ross McLean

Michael MacMillan takes a peak through the camera.

Photo : Lois Siegel

During the shooting of *Jésus de Montréal*, director Denys Arcand confessed (on the record) to Variety that the only true reason he worked in the film business was to be sure to have "plenty of extra time to play tennis and ski."

Photo : Lois Siegel

Michel Brault is known for his brilliant cinematography throughout the world. In 1975, he was honoured at the Festival international du film — commonly known as the Cannes film festival —for *Les ordres* which garnered him a best director award in the Official Competition.

Photo : Lois Siegel

Director André Forcier.

Director Denys Arcand in one of his infamous 'joie-de-vivre' poses.

Director Don Shebib on the set of *Heartaches*.

Photo : Lois Siegel

Joshua Then and Now producer Robert Lantos shares a moment with Li Fung, wife of director Ted Kotcheff.

Cinematic poet Jean-Pierre Lefebvre was one of the first auteur directors supported by the Canadian Film Development Corporation.

The late jovial Harold Greenberg built what is currently the Astral empire.

The late writer Ted Allan with producer Harry Gulkin at the 1975 Toronto premier of *Lies My Father Told Me*.

Producer Rock Demers began his 15-part family film series, *Tales for All*, after he saw *Gremlins* and was horrified by the violence. He subsequently made it his mission to produce films that children and their parents could love and enjoy.

Producer Rock Demers with Nina Petronzio, who made her screen debut in 1990 in Michael Rubbo's *Vincent and Me*, the 11th Tale For All.

Toronto director Norman Jewison at a press conference at the Montreal World
Film Festival for *Agnes of God*.

David Cronenberg directs James Spader in a scene for *Crash*, which won a Special Prize from the Cannes Jury for "audacity and originality" (Prix spécial du jury 'audace et originalité') in 1996.

Quebec's own Pierre Falardeau has directed some wonderful pictures about Canada's sometimes turbulent history such as *Octobre*.

Photo : Lois Siegel

Late director Jean-Claude Lauzon accepts a prize at the 1985 Montreal World Film Festival.

Photo : Lois Siegel

Producer Denis Héroux.

Photo : Lois Siegel

Toronto director Norman Jewison at a press conference at the Montreal World
Film Festival for *Agnes of God*.

David Cronenberg directs James Spader in a scene for *Crash*, which won a Special Prize from the Cannes Jury for "audacity and originality" (Prix spécial du jury 'audace et originalité') in 1996.

Quebec's own Pierre Falardeau has directed some wonderful pictures about Canada's sometimes turbulent history such as *Octobre*.

Late director Jean-Claude Lauzon accepts a prize at the 1985 Montreal World Film Festival.

Producer Denis Héroux.

Photo : Lois Siegel

who saw its potential for the theatres. The film had its premiere in July 1970 at the New Yorker Cinema in Toronto and played for twenty-two weeks, raking in a whopping $300,000 at the Canadian box office before its American premiere.

Following its release in 1970, *Deux femmes en or* had attracted 400,000 fans in two Montreal theatres in twenty-four weeks. By the end of its run, we calculated that almost a quarter of the population of Quebec had seen it (and it's still a staple on late-night TV in both its original French and English versions). Could Nat Taylor's dream become a reality? We must have thought so. By the time the CFDC's second annual report was issued in 1972, we confidently predicted that "there is every possibility of a feature film industry being established in Canada on a continuing basis."

I no longer rode my bicycle to the office from Hampstead, but took the commuter train from my new home in Beaconsfield to Windsor Station, a short walk to Place Victoria. A great advantage of having our office in Place Victoria was the first-class restaurant downstairs. In the spring of 1970, two senior Australian bureaucrats arrived on our doorstep to find out how an agency like the CFDC worked. I took them to lunch downstairs to learn more about how the CFDC had been generating a ripple of interest Down Under.

Barry O. Jones, the deputy chair of the Australian Arts Council, and Phillip Adams, a senior government official, asked a seemingly endless number of questions. It was impossible to answer them all, so they eventually invited me to Australia to advise them.

The Aussies treated me royally. I met their prime minister, John Gordon (he had not yet become Sir John), in the posh Hotel Canberra, and spent hours in conversation with the movers and shakers of the Australian film industry in Sydney and Melbourne. In Adelaide, the capital of the state of South Australia, which had a socialist government at the time, I must have piqued Premier Don Dunstan's interest — a year later, in 1972, he would use the information I gave him to establish the South Australia Film

Corporation. Dunstan convinced the South Australian government to go ahead with an agency to make government films in the style of the NFB and to build the studios to produce them. This was not my idea; I thought production should be done in the private sector with the government's financial support. In later years, the SAFC did become an agency with powers to invest in feature films in the private sector, like the CFDC. It was an influential investor in such Australian classics as *Breaker Morant, Sunday Too Far Away*, and *The Shirrah Lee*. From 1994 to 1999 it was even headed by a Canadian, Judith McCann, who had worked at External Affairs before joining the staff of Telefilm Canada.

I spent an evening with the Producers and Directors Guild of Australia (Melbourne Chapter), which was the breeding ground of many famous Australian filmmakers. We discussed their almost paranoid feelings about the Australian distributors and theatre owners (opinions shared by their Canadian confreres vis-à-vis the MPAA).

October 1970 resonates in the history of Quebec. Upon my arrival in Brisbane, I was shocked to open a local newspaper and read about the kidnapping of Labour Minister Pierre Laporte by the Front de Libération du Québec (FLQ) and Trudeau's subsequent imposition of the War Measures Act. The October Crisis inspired two significant Quebec films: Michel Brault and Claude Godbout's *Les ordres* in 1974, which recreated the circumstances of the police action, and twenty years later in 1994, Pierre Falardeau's *Octobre*, a dramatic reconstruction of Laporte's kidnapping and murder. Interestingly, both films received government funding despite being critical of the government's role in the crisis.

Back in Canada, the CFDC's constant priority was dealing with clients who wanted support for their feature film projects. Beyond this our concern was consulting with the industry to ensure that the actions of the Corporation and the needs of the industry coincided.

Five years earlier — at the interdepartmental committee stage, long before the CFDC Act was passed by Parliament — the committee members had realized that an effective agency would need some formal channel to get advice from the industry. As finally drafted, Section 14 of the Act created "an Advisory Group to advise the Minister and the Corporation on matters which the Minister and the Corporation may refer to it." The industry was soon lobbying the minister to make appointments to this group, but a year went by before it was established.

Among the new advisory group members were John Ross, president of the Association of Motion Picture Producers and Laboratories of Canada (AMPPLC); Robert Brooks of the Canadian Society of Cinematographers; Nat Taylor of the Motion Picture Association of Canada (MPAC); Pierre Lamy of L'association des producteurs de films du Québec, and Martin Bochner of the Canadian Motion Picture Distributors Association (CMPDA). The International Alliance of Stage Employees (IATSE) and the American Federation of Musicians (AFM) also sent delegates. Last but not least was David Cronenberg, "un jeune cinéaste indépendant de Toronto," according to the Corporation's 1969-70 annual report.

The first meeting took place in Ottawa in the early 1970s, on the fifth floor of the Government Convention Centre, formerly Union Station. This elegant building had nearly suffered demolition when the railway tracks were removed from the city, but was saved by the sheer grandeur of its facade. The marble-floored, cathedral-like concourse, however, had disappeared into offices and conference rooms.

We were concerned from the outset that the advisory group could end up functioning as simply a platform for the orators in the industry. Chairman of the first meeting, Gérard Pelletier, immediately tackled the issue. Looking around at the more than seventeen participants from all sides of the industry, he noted that "thought should be given to forming small groups within the group [distributors, theatre managers, French and English unions, etc.]. Small, specialized groups would be better able to analyze the particular problems and find solutions." Sage advice.

Later in the meeting, I observed that, our investments in thirty-nine pre-production (script) proposals notwithstanding, there was still a lack of English-language scripts good enough to extract advances from distributors. "These comments may sound negative," I went on, "but as the industry's partner and banker, I think we should point out its problems to you and get your advice." Bochner offered the CMPDA's opinion that the industry would have to produce "thirty pictures to give it the one success it needs." In other words, the more scripts, the better the chances.

As we had feared, there was very little dialogue between the participants, most of whom simply stated the views of the union or association they represented. Despite the minister's advice, we held a second plenary session two months later. It wasn't substantially different from the first, but the minutes record why this was our last attempt to hold bilingual sessions. The simultaneous translation failed and I had to apologize to the French-speaking members, "who found themselves in the necessity of listening as well as making their remarks in the English language."

Producer Roger Frappier, who has remained one of the leaders of the Quebec industry to this day, declared that "the CFDC should in no way contribute to reducing the filmmaker's creative talent to a mere level of marketing." This might have prompted André Link to say that he was "puzzled and concerned by the attitude of some members who were living in an ivory tower. They should better understand the concrete problems of the industry." "The cinema," I could easily have said to both of them, "is both an art *and* an industry."

One good result of the meeting was the decision to split the group into two sections, English and French. The agenda of the next meeting was to organize the Canadian participation at the upcoming 1971 Cannes Film Festival. This would be the second year of our participation. In the first year, with financial support from other government departments interested in external trade, the CFDC had arranged for booths with closed-circuit television set up at strategic points in the Carlton Hotel, a lavish resort on the

French Riviera and at that time the unofficial headquarters of the Cannes market. It was on its elegant beachfront terrace where some of the contracts were signed for international distribution of *Goin' Down the Road*. The film was sold to South Africa, Hungary, Holland, Norway, New Zealand, Mexico, Panama, Venezuela, Tunisia, Columbia, and Australia — a new milestone for Canadian cinema in the marketplace. The global reach of English Canadian cinema was impressive, but the nagging question was, Could we keep it up?

Since we had established the precedent of an annual meeting in Vancouver, Gélinas and I decided to go there via Los Angeles in order to meet our Hollywood contacts and find out how our Canadian pictures were faring with American distributors. We went straight to the top, meeting with Frank Davis at MGM to discuss *Fortune and Men's Eyes* and then on to see Frank Wells at Warner Bros. regarding Eric Till's *A Fan's Notes*, which was then in production. Our hosts, who saw the potential for future investments, were most gracious.

One evening Gélinas and I had dinner with Lloyd Bochner, Lorne Greene, Harvey Hart, and Norman Jewison, among other expatriate Canadians in Hollywood. We discussed the possibility of their involvement in Canadian productions, but they all had successful careers going in Los Angeles. Canadian productions were not their priority.

In Vancouver we continued our efforts to get more features produced. We had actually succeeded in getting one off the ground a year earlier. Written and directed by Morrie Ruvinsky, *The Plastic Mile* was a 16 mm production blown up to 35 mm for theatrical release. At a cost of $12,000 it must have been one of the least expensive features ever produced in Canada. Part of it was shot in Whistler, B.C., where I went on set to see Ruvinsky at work. His star, Pia Shandel, was from Vancouver and later became a well-known television talk show host. After *The Plastic Mile*, she starred in the comedy *Another Smith for Paradise*, directed by Tom Shandel.

85

Producer Jim Margellos recalls that, although the budget was $200,000, he was able to produce it for less by taking advantage of free services. There weren't many movies being made in Vancouver in those days and people were excited to be involved. One action scene took place during a parade, and rather than staging the event he put a float in a real parade. Alas — "when the film was released," Margellos said, "it only lasted one week in a downtown Vancouver cinema and I don't know what happened to it afterwards."

Nonetheless, after the CFDC's first three years, feature film productions were rolling all across Canada.

THE CFDC GETS ROLLING (1971–1972)

CHAPTER 7
SEXPLOITATION SCANDAL
1971–1972

In 1971, *The Toronto Telegram* printed this montage of *L'initiation* actress Danielle Ouimet blowing a bubble which captured Michael Spencer who was then the CFDC executive director caught in the midst of a scandal dubbed "sexploitation" by the newspaper.

By 1971 a number of Quebec-produced, CFDC-financed films had begun to draw the ire of the public. Cinépix productions like *L'initiation, Love in a Four-Letter World,* and *L'amour humain* were doing well in English-language theatres across Canada, but it seemed that whenever one of those risqué French films left Quebec screens the Corporation would get into trouble. In *The Toronto Telegram*, for instance, Betty Lee called the films "nothing more than sexploitation movies." (The photo montage that accompanied the article showed me in a soap bubble blown by actress Danielle Ouimet.)

The media soon reported that the CFDC was investing in "soft-core" pornography, and MPs began receiving letters from voters across the country. Since most of these letters made it clear that the scandal wasn't the films themselves but the fact that government money had been invested in them, MPs began to put questions to Pelletier in the House of Commons. He seemed quite relaxed about the adverse reaction, however, telling us that we could expect "quite a few poor films before you arrive at some prestigious ones." But even though the controversy wasn't affecting the box office (indeed, it seemed to be having the opposite effect), I could see that we were getting into stormy seas politically.

We felt that censoring films wasn't our responsibility. Enforcing a corporate moral position, we reasoned, would unnecessarily add another hurdle for producers to access our funds. Each province had a censor board, after all, and we didn't wish to question their decisions. On the other hand, we insisted that producers agree to any cuts the provincial boards requested.

Nonetheless, I was quickly discovering that the CFDC was exposed to attacks from people who thought federal funds shouldn't go into films of doubtful taste, even if they did make money. And some of them did: *The Initiation* (a 1969 film about university life with a lot of love scenes and very little plot), for one, returned the Corporation's investment of $72,450 and a share of the $101,723 in profits to boot. I knew from the outset that some of the films we supported wouldn't be masterpieces; *Flick* had shown us that. But the fact that government money was invested in entertainment films was now beginning to excite the critics and regularly generate headlines.

Meanwhile, Peter Strauss of Allied Artists, a Los Angeles distribution company, had learned that the CFDC was a significant investor in Cinépix's productions and came to Montreal to explore the possibility of making a deal with them. "I believe opportunities do exist in Canada which are ideal in view of Allied's philosophy and production program," he reported upon his return to Los Angeles. He continued:

> Michael Spencer, who is head of the CFDC and with whom I spent nearly four hours in what I believe to have been a mutually enjoyable exchange of ideas, is deeply troubled by the fact that he will have substantial difficulty in being able to sustain the development fund unless some success is had on both an artistic and financial level. The CFDC had financed several of the latest Cinépix ventures which are, if financially rewarding, certainly not artistic.
>
> Spencer is basically a culturally oriented politician with very little feel or understanding of market conditions or problems. He seems bright enough, however, to grasp his inadequacies in this regard and made it clear that he was hopeful of having an organization like our own to lend a bit of sophistication to their next venture.

This was typical of the discussions I had with American distribution companies. But although the CFDC was in an impossible position, at least Cinépix might stand to benefit.

Les chats bottés, a 1971 film about two lazy bachelors trying to make money and succeed with women, could not have had its premiere at a worse moment. France Film's 1970 *Deux femmes en or* had been a good-natured romp with an occasional glimpse of a breast or a behind, and it had been very popular in Québec.

Trying to duplicate this feat a year later, the Corporation supported the same team (Claude Fournier and Marie-José Raymond) on
another film, but *Les chats bottés* lacked the good humour of *Deux
femmes*. I had approved the deal with Pierre Lamy and checked the
budget carefully with Pete Legault. True to our policy of not inter-
fering on the creative side, I had taken but a cursory look at the
script.

To say Gélinas and I were dismayed when we attended the premiere of *Les chats bottés* would be putting it mildly: we were in a
state of shock. When we left the theatre and went for a coffee, we
agreed that we were facing a major crisis. It wasn't so much the
antics of the Queen Elizabeth look-alike; it was, to quote the minutes of the CFDC meeting held shortly thereafter, the "rare degree
of vulgarity" in the movie as a whole.

I recommended at that meeting that the Corporation take its
name off the title and sell its share to France Film. Some members,
however, felt that we shouldn't interfere with the commercial decision of the producers we were financing. While the critics' stings
could be politically damaging, the Quebec censor board had after all
approved the picture.

Then Pelletier weighed in. According to his own sources of
information, he told us, *Les chats bottés* was "questionable from the
point of view of a federal investment." Now, like the CBC, the
CFDC took considerable pride in its independence, and the
federal government's arm's length policy towards Crown corporations protected us from direct intervention. But it wouldn't be a
good idea, we thought, to bite the hand that fed us, and certainly
not when we were asking the Treasury Board for another $10 mil-
lion to keep operating.

In the end we decided by a majority vote to withdraw from the
picture, offering the CFDC's share to the distributor, France Film.
I sent a critical letter to the company expressing the Corporation's
considerable discontent at being associated with such tasteless junk.
The offer was declined, as it turned out, but we had at least made
the gesture.

Cabinet ministers, meanwhile, had also been reading the papers and the bad reviews of the CFDC-funded films, and told Pelletier that the next $10 million would be approved only if we were able to solve the problem. Pelletier in turn informed us in a letter that he wanted to see a real effort to improve the quality of the product; that we would need to use more readers' reports and to review scripts very carefully before making a financial commitment. Without the $10 million the Corporation could hardly stay in business, and so we assured him we had got the message: we would try to clean up our act. But that didn't mean we would get the funding any time soon. Money would be tight.

Fortunately, Carole Langlois, my former secretary, was still on staff as the Board's secretary. As someone who shared Gelinas's enthusiasm for good scripts, she was the ideal person to oversee the review of readers' reports before projects were presented to the board. She soon became the conscience of the Corporation.

Meanwhile, since the CFDC was never intended to provide 100 percent of any picture's financing, producers continued their search for other sources of funding. Among the possibilities that we had never seriously considered was the government's own tax legislation. When Montreal lawyer Don Johnston was negotiating Paul Almond's deal for his 1969 film *The Act of the Heart,* he discovered that the Canadian Income Tax Act had always allowed a tax write-off for investments in feature films produced anywhere in the world. Given that Canadian investors had been involved in U.S. features for many years, the write-off was likely instigated by American lawyers seeking tax advantages for their clients' investments.

"When I started to explore tax issues," Johnston recalls, "I realized that this could potentially be a goldmine." He subsequently took advantage of his own discoveries by launching Gendon Films, a distribution company (whose name derived from its two main partners, actress Geneviève Bujold and Don Johnston) that purchased films from the NFB for commercial distribution in Canadian theatres. One of its first films was Claude Jutra's 1970

Wow, a documentary/fantasy film about the hopes and dreams of a group of adolescents.

Tax shelters provided a meeting ground for Johnston, director-producer Denis Héroux (*Valérie*), and entrepreneur Harold Greenberg. Greenberg had acquired a major interest in a Montreal film laboratory, having profited from the small fortune he had made processing thousands of rolls of amateur film taken at Expo 67. He decided that he fit the role of movie mogul, and was soon arranging deferments of laboratory processing bills for Canadian producers.

Greenberg was a bit jealous of the success of the sexy and rebellious *Valérie*, so Héroux easily persuaded him to produce his risqué *Sept fois par jour* (1971) and Don Johnston to find the tax shelter money to finance it. Another attraction was the fact that the processing would be done in Greenberg's own lab, meaning that he could visit the projection booth to check on the nude scenes. But even though the CFDC also invested in this production, I wasn't invited to join Greenberg. Pity.

The lure of Johnston's newly discovered tax incentive was also having its effects in Toronto. David Perlmutter, a chartered accountant with show business dreams, remembers the day when John Trent, one of his clients and a film director for the CBC, said to him, "Between your business experience and my creative efforts, why don't we put together a company so that we can try to access the tax shelter?" They agreed it was an excellent idea and phoned Don Johnston in Montreal, who suggested an immediate meeting with the dynamic Greenberg.

Greenberg, Perlmutter, Trent, and Johnston got on well together. American producer Sandy Howard soon brought Perlmutter a proposal for *The Neptune Factor*, and they decided to produce it. Howard, a take-charge kind of guy who knew his business well, had been skeptical that anything existed north of the 49th parallel that could contribute to the making of a motion picture of American standards. But the ever-persuasive Greenberg managed to convince him that we had all the technical equipment and personnel he needed in Canada, and mostly in Montreal.

Ben Gazzara, Ernest Borgnine, and Yvette Mimieux — all big names at the time — were already signed to act in the picture, and Twentieth Century Fox had bought the U.S. and world rights, thus ensuring the investors a reasonable return. The CFDC decided to invest its maximum, $200,000, in the $1.5 million budget, but only after Canadian director Dan Petrie had been signed, Canadian Walter Pidgeon added to the cast, and Harold Greenberg and David Perlmutter given credit as executive producers to counterbalance Howard's producer credit. Released in 1973, *The Neptune Factor* was advertised as "the most fantastic undersea odyssey ever filmed." It was pictures like these that instituted the tradition of technical expertise in Canada. Before then, nobody thought such tricky underwater sequences could be done here.

The investment paid off. The CFDC, Perlmutter noted, "was paid back three or four years later out of the proceeds of the film." The success of *The Neptune Factor* also launched Perlmutter's company, Quadrant Films, which went on to produce director John Trent's thrillers *Heart Farm* (1970) and *Sunday in the Country* (1974) and the comedy *It Seemed Like a Good Idea at the Time* (1975), with John Candy in his first starring role in a Canadian feature film.

Meanwhile, John Bassett Jr., who had helped to finance the disastrous *Flick*, decided to try again with *Face Off* in 1971. The film — a love affair between a tough hockey player and a hippie folk singer — surely had commercial potential, and the CFDC came up with an investment. But *Face Off* failed to attract major U.S distributors, perhaps because it had no stars in its cast. The bitter truth was becoming clear: U.S. majors didn't want to distribute Canadian features, even in Canadian cinemas. For Americans to pay any attention to Canadian features they had to have big American stars, as did *The Neptune Factor*. *Face Off* just didn't make the cut.

As pressure on the CFDC built throughout the 1970s to get more films into English Canadian theatres, we had an off-the-record meeting with Pelletier. Ministers weren't supposed to influence the decisions of Crown corporations, but he had a great idea to change one of our investment policies in order to encourage the production of low-budget features. Up to then, the CFDC would invest no more than 50 percent of a film's budget, and a distribution deal had to be in place. Pelletier wanted to add the provision that if the budget was $100,000 or less, we would provide two-thirds of this sum and no longer insist on a distribution deal if the producer could find the other third from somewhere. As an added incentive, the Corporation would recover its investment only after the first third had been recouped by the private investor.

This new policy — one of the most successful programs introduced by the CFDC — gave quite a lift to the Corporation's public image and resulted in a number of new films going into production. Over the years, memorable titles included *The Hard Part Begins* (directed by Paul Lynch in 1973), *Love at First Sight* (Dan Ackroyd's first feature film, directed by Rex Bromfield in 1977), *125 Rooms of Comfort* (directed by Patrick Loubert in 1974), and the box office success *Outrageous!* (directed by Richard Benner in 1977).

During this time, however, the Corporation's power to give grants was causing a minor skirmish in the bureaucratic turf wars.

Right from its inception the CFDC had given out awards for outstanding accomplishments and offered grants to filmmakers to assist them in improving their craft. In fact, at an early Corporation meeting in 1968, we had allocated $100,000 to nine features produced before the Corporation existed: Allan King's *Warrendale*, Arthur Lamothe's *Poussière sur la ville*, Camil Adam's *Manette*, Michel Brault's *Entre la mer et l'eau douce,* Jean Pierre Lefebvre's *Il ne faut pas mourir pour ça* and *Patricia et Jean Baptiste*, Larry Kent's *High*, Gille Carle's *Le viol d'une jeune fille douce*, and Paul Almond's *Isabel.* The following year we allocated another $100,000, this time among sixty proposals submitted by filmmakers across the country. Don Shebib was one of them; his *Goin' Down the Road* received $10,000.

As could be predicted, Quebec had a different approach to the CFDC's award policy. Some Montreal filmmakers were opposed to the idea of anyone other than filmmakers deciding how CFDC award money should be spent. Producers Marc Daigle and Roger Frappier suggested to us that, rather than hold a competition for individual merit, the Corporation should make a single grant to a new co-operative that they would establish. The co-operative, which they assured us would be truly representative of all the filmmakers in Montreal, would decide on its own how the money should be allocated. We accepted the idea, and thus was born L'association co-operative des producteurs audio-visuels (ACPAV) with a $50,000 grant.

"We used the money to put a structure in place and basically keep on doing what we were doing," Daigle said. I recall two films from that era: *Bulldozer* by Pierre Harel and *La vie rêvée*, the first feature film produced in the private sector directed by a woman, Mireille Dansereau. The ACPAV still exists today as a producing entity — and Daigle is still there too.

Although the co-operative idea faded as more filmmakers made individual applications to the Corporation, at the beginning it was a good example of how the CFDC, with its small staff and bicultural approach, was able to deal with the two solitudes in entirely different ways, apparently to the satisfaction of both.

The grant skirmish, however, was getting more serious. The Canada Council fired a warning shot across our bow: giving grants to artists was its affair, and we were encroaching. Furthermore, since our methods were unconventional and even haphazard (we once paid for an aspiring cameraman to spend three weeks training in Los Angeles on the basis of a brief conversation I had with him), the Council urged Pelletier to rein us in on this front. He did just that, and we weren't allowed to give grants after the end of the 1970–71 fiscal year — a tactical advance for the Canada Council in the ongoing bureaucratic wars.

Another thorny issue arose for the fledgling CFDC in 1971. We had discovered that spending money on pre-production did not necessarily result in completed productions. Many projects never got to the final script stage (never mind production), and getting a scenario to the point where it could be considered for a significant investment was costly. Since we had only limited resources, we often turned down proposals that we thought producers should develop themselves. But many talented writers and directors who wanted us to support them had absolutely no confidence in any producers. Torn between the desire to support worthy scripts and the difficulty of getting them into production, we did fund at least a few producer-less scripts. One of them was 1972's *The Rowdyman*, a film about the antics of a small-town drunk written by and starring Gordon Pinsent.

Pinsent was among the many Canadians who had decamped to Hollywood in search of better opportunities. Although by this time he was doing quite well there, he had read about the new CFDC and sent us a script he had been working on between assignments. Strangely enough, the sandy beaches of the Pacific Ocean had somehow inspired him to write of the rocky shores of his homeland.

The lack of a producer and director was a concern, but once we gave him the funds Pinsent was able to recruit Peter Carter in the latter role. I recommended my friend Budge Crawley, who had been part of our European delegation in 1965and had since independently produced *The Luck of Ginger Coffey* and *Amanita Pestilens*, as executive producer.

I myself had long since abandoned all hopes of being a producer, but when a project like *The Rowdyman* came along, I couldn't stay away. I visited the location in Corner Brook, ostensibly to keep an eye on Crawley, Pinsent, and Carter, who suggested I make myself useful by being an extra in a bar scene. (I didn't even finish up on the cutting room floor.) I also had the pleasure of going to *The Rowdyman*'s world premiere in Ottawa, with Prime Minister Trudeau and his wife Margaret in attendance. (Premieres were another real perk amid the endless meetings in the boardroom of Place Victoria.) *The Rowdyman* is still one of the Corporation's success stories, occasionally showing up on late-night television.

Although we were trying to move in the direction of Canadian stories, many Canadian filmmakers wanted to use American scripts and actors in order to draw a larger audience. Eric Till, who in 1968 had directed the Canadian story *A Great Big Thing* about a young man's aimless life, was now directing *A Fan's Notes*, based on an American novel. A major U.S. star at the time, Jerry Orbach, had been cast in the leading role. The Canadian content, however, was sufficient to justify the maximum $200,000 CFDC investment: the producer, Peter Carter (who had directed *The Rowdyman*), was Canadian; the film was shot in the Toronto area; Toronto laboratories and sound recording facilities were used; and the people behind the camera (along with most of the other performers, including actress Patricia Collins and cinematographer Harry Makin) were Canadian.

At the same time, Gilles Carle's *La vraie nature de Bernadette* (1972), the story of a liberated woman who leaves the city to practise a less conventional lifestyle, was also in production, and *Kamouraska* (1973), a historical romance based on Anne Hébert's classic Quebec novel, was being directed by Claude Jutra. I recommended that we reserve $250,000 for the latter — $50,000 over the Corporation's ceiling in those days — because I wanted to encourage leading producers like Pierre Lamy to make pictures of high quality. This was also the year that Jean-Pierre Lefevbre followed his 1970 film, *Q-bec — My Love* (which focused on the appeal of sexually titilating films, and was a surprising commercial success), with the 1971 drama *Les maudits sauvages*, about a trapper and a young Aboriginal woman. And Denys Arcand made his 1972 directorial debut with *La maudite galette*, the story of a poor Montreal plumber who turns to murdering his uncle.

Since we'd had such a positive experience at the Cannes Film Festival in 1970, Gélinas and I headed up the Canadian delegation in 1971. In a far more organized and efficient manner, we arranged to screen films in the market and to help Canadian producers to make sales where we could. Among that year's films was Harold Greenberg and Denis Héroux's Canada/Israel unofficial co-production *Sept fois par jour*, another sexy film about an architect's irrepressible urge to seduce every young woman he encounters (and the latest installment in the trend described by *Variety* as "maple syrup porno").

My trip to the Cannes festival included one rather unnerving encounter. Canadians Murray Shostak and Gerry Potterton had developed the animated and live-action feature *Tiki-Tiki*. They had acquired the rights to the Russian children's film of the same name from Commonwealth United Entertainment, an American distributor, and were now ready to present their version to international buyers at Cannes. But the original Russian creator of the movie hadn't been informed that anyone was going to make a new version of it, and so when he was invited to the same screening as the rest of us, he was understandably furious. After it was over he stalked down the aisle — and chose me as a suitable target for his rage. I thought I could hear the word "desecration" in the venomous mix of Russian and English spilling from his mouth.

Ivan Reitman's bizarre comic-horror film *Cannibal Girls* was another Canadian film shopping for a distributor at Cannes that year. Reitman had completed the film without financial assistance from the CFDC — a fact he made good use of in a 1973 interview with the Canadian film magazine *Take One*. The interview is a good example of Reitman's ironic sense of humour. He didn't mention that the CFDC came up with the money for *Foxy Lady*, his previous lacklustre feature, but he certainly felt that we used poor judgment in turning down *Cannibal Girls*. He and Dan Goldberg, his co-producer, had even worked out a strategy to deal with us. "We thought the best way to impress the CFDC would be to show up wearing nothing but barrels. We wanted to impress on them how broke we were. . . . Another approach was to write a whole lot of phony screening reports in order to convince them that a lot of people had seen the film and thought it was great." We knew nothing of this — if indeed it was true — and felt justified in rejecting the project. (Would we have changed our minds if we had known what was going on as reported in *Take One*? I doubt it.) In the same article, Reitman said the CFDC turned the picture down because it was not commercial enough! (I doubt that I ever said any such thing.) "What?" Reitman expostulated. "A film called *Cannibal Girls* is not commercial enough?" In his always dramatic fashion, he added, "Among other things, we were actually being threatened physically by one of our creditors who had connections with the Mafia."

The CFDC did do him one favour though, by getting the film out of French Customs just in time for a screening in Cannes with Sam Arkoff, the head of American International Pictures. ("The Corporation was very good at things like that," Reitman admits.) And *Cannibal Girls* eventually went on to make quite a lot of money for Cinépix as well as American International Pictures. Eventually, no doubt, Reitman got his fees out of the picture. (The CFDC never did receive any return on *Foxy Lady*.)

The Cannes festival had made us aware of just how important festivals and award shows were in promotion. Thinking that the Canadian Film Awards could provide a similar launching pad for Canadian features, we kept an eye on it with this in mind.

The awards were inaugurated in 1949, when the NFB was still in Ottawa, when the CBC wasn't producing films at all, and when the private sector, at least on the English side, was only thinking about its potential. By 1978, recognizing Canada's bicultural creative roots, the awards metamorphosed into the Genies, the Geminis, and the Gemeaux — the latter pair for English and French television respectively, while the Genies remained open to Canadian films in both English and French. Very soon, however, the French-language Jutra Awards were inaugurated in Montreal to compete with the Genies, maintaining the tradition of cultural dichotomy in Canada. In 1971 the Canadian Film Awards gave most of its statuettes to Claude Jutra's NFB film *Mon oncle Antoine*, about a young boy coming of age in rural Quebec. It was a choice, we thought, that boded well for his upcoming release, *Kamouraska*.

The film's win was partly attributable to Sydney Newman, who had been appointed film commissioner in 1970 and whom Jutra had consulted extensively at the editing stages. I had known Newman for years; after the Second World War he and I were colleagues in the production division of the NFB. When Arthur Irwin came on the scene and appointed Donald Mulholland director of production, Newman saw that he had a limited future at the NFB. He persuaded Irwin to send him to New York, where he could learn television production at NBC. From there he went to the U.K., where he first became the director of television drama for Granada and then assumed the same role at the BBC.

Newman was a creative producer in the very best sense of the word. He had an international reputation and could have pursued his career in the U.S. or the U.K., where he would have had money and the resources of a sophisticated cadre of writers, directors, set designers, and performers. Nevertheless, when he completed this contract he decided to return to Canada. In a letter Newman wrote to me when he was in the U.K. he expressed his real desire to return to his native roots. He spoke of the strong feelings he had retained, from working with John Grierson, about the place of Canada in the world and the role of the documentary filmmaker.

No wonder that when Newman was offered the role of film commissioner at the NFB, he leapt at the chance. Unfortunately, things had changed since he had been Grierson's admiring acolyte. It was no longer possible for the film commissioner to also function as its chief producer. Perhaps it was his frustration with the NFB that caused Newman to harangue the other members of the CFDC (of which he was an ex-officio member) about the poor quality of the pictures it was financing. At one meeting in those days he remarked, "The only thing to do with this organization is to close it down and give all money to the National Film Board. It can certainly do a better job."

I understood Sydney's frustration; he was a film producer, not a cultural bureaucrat. That was my role.

SEXPLOITATION SCANDAL (1971–1972)

CHAPTER 8
CANADA TOASTS CANNES
1972–1974

Gilles Carle's *La vraie nature de Bernadette* marked Canada's first privately produced feature in Cannes' Official Competition in 1972. This photo features Quebec stars Donald Pilon and Micheline Lanctôt.

In 1972, Gérard Pelletier persuaded the Treasury Board to provide the CFDC with a second $10 million, despite the setback of *Les chats bottés*. Almost simultaneously, we found ourselves toasting Canada's first privately produced feature films in the Official Competition at the *Festival international du film* in Cannes, commonly known in English as the Cannes film festival. Five years after the CFDC's birth, the international film community was taking Canadian features seriously. The festival's selection committee had chosen two films — *A Fan's Notes* by Eric Till and *La vraie nature de Bernadette* by Gilles Carle — for the world's most important festival competition, a Canadian record at the time.

Intent on planning a celebration worthy of the occasion, we booked the Casino restaurant, in those days just across the street from the Grand Palais Theatre where the films in competition were screened. Our guest list included all the VIPs at the festival as well as the Canadian ambassador in Paris. And, since this was to be a Canadian party, we thought we should serve a Canadian delicacy.

Gratien Gélinas's wife, Huguette Oligny, acted as our culinary consultant. She knew where we could get the very best smoked salmon in Quebec; it would be shipped in by air the day before the reception. All was moving along smoothly until the Casino's head chef called on the morning of the big dinner. The chef was not going to serve our smoked salmon. He had inspected it upon its arrival, decided that it was not as good as the local fare, and insisted that his reputation would suffer if he served ours. Upset at this slight, Gélinas, Madame Oligny, and I jumped in a taxi to the Casino.

A hot-tempered dialogue ensued between Madame Oligny and the chef, during which she asked him to produce his own smoked salmon. This he did with a big smile. How could any sensible person not agree that it was much better than the import?

Madame Oligny was superb in her rejection of what she called "lox" in scornful tones. After further discussion the chef reluctantly backed down, but pointed out that he did not know how to cut it properly. Madame Oligny seized a knife and showed him how. And so it was that the Gaspé delicacy was served later in the evening, to compliments all around. (We allowed the chastened chef to take credit for a great innovation to French cuisine, the "Gaspé Smoked Salmon" that appeared on each gold-tasselled menu.)

Another contretemps had meanwhile resulted after one of my staff, Christian Rasselet, hired a couple of actors to wear the RCMP uniforms he had rented in Paris for the occasion. They would be standing at attention at either end of a row of ten flag-poles, each flying the flag of a province. This patriotic tableau was arranged for the main entrance of the Casino on the night the Canadian entry was to be shown. On the evening before, Rasselet put on one of the uniforms and went for a stroll in the lobby of the Carlton hotel. The film critics for *La Presse* and *Le Devoir* (Luc Perreault and Jean-Pierre Tadros) ran into him by chance, and both wrote stories to underline how scandalous it was that the RCMP (a foreign symbol, as they saw it) should be used to promote Quebec movies. Once again I was reminded that a Canadian cultural bureaucrat was there to serve two hegemonies, even if one is totally opposed to the dreams and aspirations of the other.

The black-tie audience warmly welcomed *La vraie nature de Bernadette*, and after the screening Gilles Carle and his star Micheline Lanctôt were met with plenty of applause and a barrage of flash bulbs as they walked down the red-carpeted steps to the palm-lined Croisette. A limousine and a line of cars waited to take the stars and VIPs to the party at the Casino. Lanctôt was the first to arrive at the bottom of the stairs and naturally assumed the limousine was for her. The chauffeur opened the door, but once she was inside he informed her that the limousine was, in fact, for Léo Cadieux, the Canadian ambassador. She was asked to get out. At this moment my old friend, producer Pierre Lamy, and Gilles Carle arrived to witness Lanctôt stepping back onto the red carpet. Lamy was furious at the way his star had been treated and let the chauffeur know it before storming off to the casino on foot with Lanctôt, Carles, and Donald Pilon in tow. Upon arrival they discovered the ambassador at the front of the receiving line. "We breezed right past him and declined to shake his hand," Lanctôt recalled with a smile.

Nonetheless, the celebration at the Casino was a great success. Robert Charlebois entertained us with a selection of his Québécois songs, and we wrapped up the evening with a splendid fireworks display in the garden just outside the windows of the restaurant.

A Fan's Notes screened at the end of the festival, when most of the international guests and press had gone. Gratien Gélinas, Eric Till, and I attended the screening, but we had no excuse to throw another party. And while the publicity was still sufficient to prompt Warner Bros. to fund a decent release for the film in Toronto, sadly, it did not do significant business either there or in the U.S.

The federal election that fall returned the Liberals to power, though with a minority, and heralded the appointment of a new secretary of state, Hugh Faulkner. A Montrealer by birth, Faulkner had become a schoolteacher in Peterborough, Ontario, where he had once given an impressive speech at a Rotary Club luncheon. This caught the attention of the local Liberal riding association looking for a candidate. As Faulkner told it many years later:

> I went to the headmaster and said: "Listen, I've been offered a chance to run." He surprised me by saying approvingly: "That's a good idea and I'll tell you why. I'm a Conservative. You're going to lose. But the activity you're going to generate by being in an election is going to be of more value to the students than anything you can possibly teach them. So go ahead!" He was dead right. I lost, but eventually won in 1965.

Faulkner soon became parliamentary secretary to Gérard Pelletier. "We had a good personal and, most particularly, a professional relationship," he recalled. "Particularly in terms of Quebec, he was as good a sounding board, as good a colleague as one could hope for. I kept in close touch with him."

The head of a government agency — particularly a Crown corporation — waits anxiously for his first meeting with the new minister. I was no exception. As I waited in his office on Elgin Street I noticed the familiar painting by Jean-Paul Lemieux that I had admired in the days when Pelletier was the minister I was meeting.

My intention was to get Faulkner's support for a Cabinet memorandum, which we had been working on for some time and which would make the CFDC an agency with some clout. The memorandum proposed that the government should:

> (A) Agree to the Corporation's direct involvement in the distribution of Canadian feature films
>
> (B) Take all possible measures to assist in the establishment of a third chain of motion picture theatres
>
> (C) Support the increases in money and personnel, which the CFDC will need to carry out its increased responsibility in distribution
>
> (D) Assist the Corporation: (1) in its negotiations with the provinces concerning a box-office levy and possible quota and (2) in organizing a meeting to discuss short films with the exhibition and distribution industry
>
> (E) Formally approach the Minister of Finance in connection with the existing duties and withholding tax as they are presently applied to the Canadian film industry
>
> (F) Take the necessary measures to place any required changes in the CFDC Act on the legislative calendar

These recommendations hadn't come out of thin air; they were the result of several meetings the Corporation had held over the past year with members of the industry through its advisory group. They also had the full support of Gérard Pelletier, the previous secretary of state and now the minister of Communications. And I was delighted to find out that our new minister was on our side.

At this point my life took a dramatically different turn. My marriage ended and my wife and youngest daughter, Teresa-Jane, moved to Toronto while I moved to Nun's Island with my other daughter, Christina. Shortly thereafter Jim Beveridge, my long-time colleague from the NFB, introduced me to a fascinating woman from Hyderabad, India. Maqbool Jung made an instant and lasting impression on me, and we have been inseparable ever since.

Meanwhile, the CFDC continued with its main purpose, which was to invest money in Canadian feature films. If we weren't busy reviewing scripts and checking budgets, we were going to shoots, viewing rough cuts, or attending premieres — each year we were involved in more than fifty films. Three of these stand out in my memory.

Quelques arpents de neige, directed by Denis Héroux and produced by Claude Héroux, was shot on Ile Perrot, near Montreal. The script called for irregular Quebec freedom fighters on horseback to attack the British in a cavalry charge across ice not strong enough to support the horses, which would be plunged into the water and drowned. I was curious to see how they were going to get the shot, but when I went on location for this spectacular scene I discovered that it was easier than I'd thought. It was filmed on a part of the lake where the horses could rapidly regain their footing about one foot below the ice and off camera; horses and riders were unharmed and ready for the close-ups that were shot later. It was a very convincing scene, especially for a film with an entire budget of $500,000. Although it was uncomfortable standing around in the cold, being on location gave me a chance to meet the people who were doing the hard work of actually making the movie — including director of photography Bernard Chentrier, soundman Joseph Champagne, whom I knew from the NFB, and Claude Léger, then doing his first job as a production manager.

Alien Thunder, intended as a tribute to the RCMP on the occasion of its 100th anniversary in 1973, was exceptional for many reasons that had nothing to do with the quality of the picture. Marie-José Raymond and Claude Fournier had found the perfect "always gets its man" story in the RCMP archives and asked W.O. Mitchell to write the screenplay. The film starred Gordon Tootoosis as

Almighty Voice, a Cree who had been accused of murder and who was pursued and eventually caught by the RCMP's Constable Dan Candy (Donald Sutherland).

The RCMP agreed to provide the horses and riders and $250,000 towards the $1 million budget. Paul Desmarais of Power Corporation was approached to sponsor the production by sharing the cost with MGM, which had already been approached by Raymond and Fournier and had liked W.O. Mitchell's script. MGM offered to pick up the film for $500,000 and was also willing to help with its expertise in the location shooting, especially in the scenes involving cannons, explosions, cavalry charges, and troop movements. All the elements for success were in place.

The CFDC wasn't asked to participate, so I was deprived of what could have been an interesting location visit when Almighty Voice was finally overwhelmed by a large force of Mounties. In the end, the film was overwhelmed, too. Mitchell withdrew, disagreeing with script changes. MGM withdrew because it couldn't make a deal with Power Corp. The commissioner of the RCMP at the time didn't like the film and withdrew its support. The distributor, Cinerama Releasing, went broke and the original negative of the film has disappeared. Two prints remain in the public Canadian archives.

The third film was *Lies My Father Told Me*, directed by Czech Jan Kadar and produced by Harry Gulkin. Incredibly, Gulkin had purchased the rights to Ted Allan's play for a mere one dollar. They were in a pub in London called The White Elephant, which happened to have a casino on its top floor. Allan disappeared from the table only to return an hour later flat broke. "He lost everything he had, so I paid for the dinner," Gulkin told me. "And I got the option."

That was only the beginning. There were many slips between the cup and lip before Columbia saved the day with the last $100,000 and released the film in New York and Montreal to excellent reviews. By this time the CFDC had invested $220,000 of the final $1.1 million budget, and I told Gulkin he wasn't getting one more cent. "You were very cold, Michael, and very suspicious and with good reason," he recalled.

From the time of the interdepartmental committee we had been convinced that quotas and tax levies were the best means available to further our ambitions for homegrown Canadian movies. We had never lost sight of the fact that, with the exception of the American juggernaut, all film industries had survived thanks to protective measures introduced by governments to restrict the flow of foreign films. Since the provinces had jurisdiction over theatres, we felt that they should use the entertainment tax on cinema tickets to create a special fund to invest in the production of Canadian films. The feedback we had from our own contacts in the industry through our advisory group impressed upon us that the time had come for quotas and levies. Hugh Faulkner seemed to be in agreement with this approach:

> The key to it is to get money into the industry in a way that allows the development of the juices required, then just confront the market forces out there. Now that's a more difficult thing in Canada because we've got exactly the same language. With ten times, even forty times more money to play with, and the star appeal of Los Angeles, it's hard to compete out of Toronto, Montreal, or Vancouver. And the only way you could do it is by becoming so bloody good in your own backyard that you attract good people. I think that's the only philosophical basis for public policy on culture.

About two years earlier Faulkner had successfully introduced the idea of taxing the Canadian advertising revenues of the Canadian editions of *Time* and *Reader's Digest*, but it hadn't been easy. "Even in Cabinet, there were difficulties," he remembered. "Bud Drury, Warren Allmand, and others had constituencies in Montreal ridings. That's where *Reader's Digest* had its plant. There was no enthusiasm for this bill."

"Prime Minister Trudeau was terrifically patient," Faulkner added. "I remember we were flying back from a dinner and he said, 'Where are we with this bill? What am I going to say to President

Ford tomorrow?' And I said, 'Prime Minister, just tell them that it's on track and that there's growing support in the country.' He smiled and said: 'That's probably enough. I'll try to get off that subject as quickly as possible.' Trudeau was terrific."

Quotas would guarantee Canadian pictures a percentage of Canadian screen time; levies would ensure that a slice of the box office pie would be reserved for Canadian producers. The provinces held the power to institute both, and we had to approach them directly.

Armed with a brief — which had Faulkner's approval — Peter Roberts, the assistant undersecretary of state for Cultural Affairs; Jo Beaubien, the Corporation's in-house lawyer; and I visited every province in order to make our pitch. And while they were reluctant to impose levies, every one of them supported the principle of quotas.

Professional associations like the 7,000-member Council of Canadian Filmmakers also jumped on the bandwagon. Peter Pearson, its combative president, attacked the federal government for its failure to put quotas in place to protect the Canadian industry. "A crisis can be an opportunity," he declared. The Toronto Filmmakers Co-op weighed in with a brief, and filmmakers across the country let it be known that they, too, believed federal action was needed. Proposed quotas and levies were making headlines. Momentum was growing for the creation of a production fund for Canadian pictures.

The Motion Picture Association of America saw the headlines and swung into action, contacting Canadian politicians through theatre managers with the message that American features were much more popular than Canadian pictures could ever be. Millard Roth, executive director of the Canadian Association of Motion Pictures Distributors, had been well briefed by MPAA president Jack Valenti and insisted that any attempt to curtail the free-market distribution of American movies in Canada would be a very bad political move. The lobbying campaign had some effect.

Recalling these events, Hugh Faulkner said: "People were telling me I should see Jack Valenti, and I said that's a total waste of my time and it's a waste of his time. He doesn't give a damn about Canadian film."

Meanwhile, conscious of the growing public interest, the Ontario government had appointed a task force under John F. Bassett. Its report, tabled in January 1973, reinforced the lobbying for quotas and levies. Bassett, the producer of *Paperback Hero* and *Face Off* and a young man in a hurry, was a good choice to head the task force. He knew how the market was biased against Canadian producers, and was able to persuade the other members of the task force to agree with the recommendation that "a quota system combined with a bonus incentive program for Ontario theatres would develop audiences for Ontario-made feature films and significantly increase the inflow of dollars into the Ontario film industry to the benefit of all associated with feature film production."

The Bassett report included the novel idea of "forcing" exhibitors to conduct test-market screenings in order to "test the profitability of Canadian films in the marketplace rather than in private screening rooms where they are subject to the prejudices of too many years of experience." The idea, unsurprisingly, wasn't much appreciated by Famous Players and Odeon. The Ontario government itself reacted to the report with faint praise and did nothing to implement the recommendations.

Added to the mix was the infamous loophole in tax policy. The National Revenue Department was naturally not in favour of Don Johnston's initiatives, and began reviewing proposals with a fine-tooth comb, making it difficult to invest private money in feature films. Such a battle is a constant theme in the development of any industry. Lawyers and accountants advise their clients on how to take advantage of whatever tax savings are possible; officials in National Revenue try to maximize the government's income.

Our lawyer, Jo Beaubien, was well aware of these tactics and, like me, thought the department was being unreasonable. There was no point, we felt, in producing Canadian feature films if they didn't receive a greater tax advantage than foreign features. And so we were working on a proposal to Hugh Faulkner recommending that if a picture was certified as Canadian (and we would do the certification, as called for in the CFDC Act), it should be allowed a capital cost allowance of 100 percent.

In the spring of 1973 National Revenue made its move. It disallowed tax rebates on any amounts that had not been invested in films in the form of cash (non-recourse loans would be ineligible). Undersecretary of State Jean Boucher carried the bad news to a meeting of the producer's association in Ste. Adele, stating categorically that the industry could no longer count on tax loopholes to finance Canadian feature films. He added that this form of financing would create the wrong image of the film industry; *parasitaire* was the word he used.

The announcement made headlines. Private money, most comfortable in the shadows, began to hold back and our hoped-for source of funds for the Canadian film industry was in trouble. A serious lack of private money in the industry would make it impossible for the CFDC to fulfill its mandate. Both *The Globe and Mail* and *The Toronto Star* reported that the slowing down of feature film production was due to a hardline policy in the National Revenue Department.

The industry and its lawyers, particularly Don Johnston, considered this a minor setback, however. It wasn't long before they discovered other loopholes, and tax money continued to flow into Canadian feature films.

In the midst of all this political turmoil and lobbying, the demands on our limited resources continued to increase. Nineteen features with total budgets of $7 million were produced in 1973, with the Corporation investing 37 percent of their budgets. We were usually asked to invest more than 50 percent, which was strictly against our guidelines. If we wouldn't do that, producers hoped that we would agree to recover our investment after everyone else had been paid back. Hugh Faulkner was pushing National Revenue on the 100 percent CCA, but it hadn't yet been approved.

At the same time, Finance was on our back and we were trying to stay below a ceiling of $3.5 million for that fiscal year, including $600,000 from returns on our investments. The industry had to get money from somewhere.

I had persuaded Faulkner to meet with the presidents of Famous Players and Odeon to negotiate a voluntary quota agreement that would guarantee a minimum of two weeks' screening time for any Canadian film they booked in any theatre they controlled. We also wanted them to invest in Canadian features. George Destounis had earlier agreed to this, of course, which probably convinced Chris Salmon of Odeon to go along with the deal, despite having refused the year before. Faulker remembers that Destounis was helpful:

> He understood where we were coming from. He had his problems because the American side really didn't care at all about the Canadian feature film business. For them, it was a minor sort of irritant. Destounis was sort of caught between them and me, and I thought he handled it with considerable skill. He gave me a push to get me started but didn't go overboard to engage us in a major battle with the Americans.

That agreement was a promising step. And more good news was to come from audience numbers. The key indicator of the Corporation's progress was always at the box office: the CFDC had come into existence to put Canadian films on Canadian theatre screens, and the number of box office receipts was a good measuring stick. Our Quebec-based productions rapidly went to the top of the charts there, so we knew we were fulfilling our mandate in that province. Our star director that year was Denis Héroux, whose *J'ai mon voyage*, a comedy about a French Canadian family driving across Canada, earned $500,000 in Quebec theatres. Jean-Claude Lord followed closely in 1974 with his well-received drama *Bingo*, the story of a young photographer caught in a terrorist plot. His first feature in 1972, *Les colombes*, had returned its CFDC investment and was making a profit. Bingo indeed.

All these films were distributed in Quebec by Pierre David's dynamic new company, Les films mutuelles. David recalls:

> One day, Jean-Claude Lord came to see me and he had a project called *Les colombes*. It was going to be made for less than one hundred thousand dollars. Very, very low budget. That was my first Quebec movie. I remember these incredible moments of going to see you and your team. I'll always remember that day when Jean-Claude Lord started crying in the conference room because there were all kinds of problems. He said: "I've worked so hard to put this together." Which was true. I remember you taking me aside and saying: "I can't let a guy cry like this about his project. He's so dedicated. Let's give him the bloody money. Let's make it simple. You got it. Get out of my office."
>
> And that was the first Jean-Claude Lord movie; it was a very big success. It was the first movie that I got involved in to raise money. That was my first experience of working with you.

Meanwhile, some English-language feature films finally showed significant signs of life. *Wedding in White* (William Fruet's 1972 gothic horror movie) and *The Rowdyman* had enjoyed successful theatrical releases and generally good reviews. *The Neptune Factor* had earned $2.3 million in the U.S., the U.K., and several other countries.

And international film festivals, we were beginning to see, could function as springboards for Canadian films that couldn't even get into the theatres in Canada. In the 1973 Cannes Competition we had another film by Gilles Carle, *La mort d'un bûcheron*, which starred Carole Laure as a young girl taken advantage of while searching for her father and which was very well received. In September we were flattered by a week of Canadian cinema in Sorrento, Italy; other festivals were also inviting Canadian feature films.

But we were still facing our perennial problem. The English-language films weren't making much money at home, and even less abroad. We were pleased by the results of *The Only Way Out Is Dead* (originally *The Heart Farm*) and *Fortune and Men's Eyes*. Even *Les mâles* and *La vraie nature de Bernadette* had made a decent showing. But the frustrating part was that our best Quebec successes, such as *Kamouraska, J'ai mon voyage,* and *Bingo* — which were enthusiastically received in Quebec — hardly made a dent in foreign distribution. *The Pyx,* a 1973 horror film about a devil-worshipping cult, produced by Maxine Samuels, and *Paperback Hero* (1972), about a small-town hockey player who has delusions of being a gunslinger, directed by Peter Pearson, earned good money ($650,000 and $632,000, respectively), but this put insignificant amounts in the producers' pockets after the theatres had taken their 50 percent and the distributors deducted their fees and paid for prints and advertising.

Our man in Toronto, Chalmers Adams, had long wanted to be a producer and I began looking around for someone to replace him. I found a good candidate in Ted Rouse. He recalled how I told him he had the job: "I got this phone call. It was a very official British voice: 'The Corporation has decided to offer you a job.' I was so taken aback! I thought it was a friend of mine playing a prank."

Among the projects he convinced me to invest in was *Power Play,* produced by Robert Cooper (who became a very successful producer at HBO) and starring Peter O'Toole. I thought the script was rather weak and I wanted to pass. Rouse thought I was being rash:

> You basically said to Cooper: "I really don't like you and I don't like your project." And I said: "Michael, for heaven's sake!" Cooper then said very politely: "I have a good reason to tell you to go to hell." And you said: "That's fine then." And that was the end of the meeting. In the elevator Bob was having a fit. He was in tears. He said: "I just completely screwed up my whole career." On the way home to Toronto I thought he was going to jump out of the airplane!

Ultimately, Rouse managed to change my mind. He was either very convincing or I was easily influenced. One thing I learned as a cultural bureaucrat was that each project had to be considered as a whole and if it was any good we would invest in it. My personal feelings didn't count.

117

To have a functioning industry we had to make money, and the money, we knew, was in television. But six months earlier when we requested this extension to our Act, we were rebuffed. It had seemed to us that the Corporation should have the power to invest in films of any running time, including television films and series. Peter Roberts and I prepared a memorandum to Cabinet on the subject, and its committee on communications had agreed to hear our brief. We made our case based on the television market, which was obviously going to be huge. To my surprise, however, the committee chairman, Gérard Pelletier, turned us down on the basis of the CFDC's own success. (He was obviously thinking of the popularity that CFDC-funded features had enjoyed in Quebec.) With so many people flocking to the theatres, the committee reasoned, who needed television? It would take another fifteen years for the Corporation to be legally entitled to invest in TV.

Toward the end of 1973 I had a golden opportunity to extend the reach of Canadian feature films into India. My second wife, Maqbool Jung, had been a film journalist in India before she immigrated to Canada in 1967. Through her many contacts with the Indian film industry I had received an invitation from the Ministry of Information and Broadcasting in New Delhi to bring a delegation from the Canadian film industry to India to open the market for Canadian features there. The cost of moving us around would be borne by the Indian government. Without consulting External, a grave error of protocol, the Corporation accepted the offer. Our little delegation consisted of Gilles Carle, Carol Laure, and Maqbool and me— and a selection of Canadian films, of course.

On our way to India, Maqbool and I stopped for a week at the Second International Film Festival of Iran. The Shah was still in power of course, and we were treated like royalty, as were other guests of the festival, among whom were Gregory Peck, James Mason, Ann Miller, and Christopher Lee. The festival ensured that we saw not only Iranian and foreign films, but some of the country's most beautiful cities, including Shiraz, Persepolis, and Isfahan.

(Standing in the main square of Isfahan with its surrounding blue mosques is like being transported to the glories of ancient Muslim empires.) In keeping with the pomp and glamour of the old regime, Queen Farah herself presented the awards at the closing ceremonies.

As I watched from my seat in the balcony an interesting situation arose. The Diplomatic Corps was seated in the front rows of the theatre, with the filmmakers behind them. When the award for Best Animation Film was announced, the ambassador of the country concerned rose at the same time as the filmmaker several rows behind him. The ambassador was unaware of this, but the filmmaker hastened up the aisle, determined to receive the prize himself from the hand of Queen Farah. Both arrived at the same time. I was pleased that the ambassador graciously gave way to the filmmaker.

When we arrived at the Bombay airport we met Laure and Carle and were garlanded by our hosts. Bombay, now known officially as Mumbai, is the famous "Bollywood" film capital of India. At the time, India was producing more films per year than any other country; its populace has an insatiable movie appetite, especially for musicals.

Carole Laure, the star of our delegation, was followed everywhere by admiring crowds. Carle and I were invited to see several Indian movies which, with their songs and typical three-hour running times, were not exactly what we were accustomed to. We also met with the officers of the NFDC, the Indian version of the CFDC. Among the stars of Indian cinema, we met Raj Kapoor, Sunil Dutt, and Dev Anand.

The seven Canadian features (and twelve shorts) that were showcased received lots of publicity and plenty of parties during our two-week stay. Carle's *La mort d'un bûcheron* made the cover page of *Screen*, self-billed as the "largest certified net sales among all film weeklies in India."

In a comical piece headlined "Friendship — Indian Style," the scribe wrote:

> The reception hosted by the All India Film Producers' Council last Sunday in Bombay in honour of the visiting four-member Canadian film delegation was enlivened by the witticisms of our inimitable I.S. Johar.
>
> The funster, in his usual tongue-in-cheek Joharian way, said "I am a known plagiarist. So far, I have drawn inspiration from American and British films. Now your Canadian films have inspired me. And, before long, if you find in your country an Indian movie titled *Death of an Indian Lumberjack*, do not be surprised, or try to sue me for plagiarism like some American companies have done recently, for that is not our idea of friendship between nations."

While we thoroughly enjoyed India's hospitality, I was dismayed that the audience for our Canadian features turned out to be mostly men who thought Canadian films were porno. (Had they been reading *The Toronto Telegram?* Had they heard rumours about *Valérie?*)

But there was no doubt that we'd been taken seriously when Prime Minister Indira Gandhi requested an interview with us at her residence in Delhi. We were graciously received and questioned about the CFDC and the Canadian film industry. Gandhi also knew a lot about the NFB and John Grierson, and when she subsequently visited Canada she specially requested a visit to the Board.

I returned to Canada shortly before the Corporation's yearly meeting in Vancouver. Our annual report for 1973–74 had just been issued, listing only two pictures from the West, and we were attacked by Les Wedman of *The Vancouver Sun* for not paying enough attention to West Coast filmmakers. (He didn't seem to understand how things worked. It wasn't up to us to ask them if they wanted the money; they had to ask us.) We had two more films by Vancouver directors planned for that year: Boone Collins's western comedy, *Sally Fieldgood*, and Peter Bryant's comedy *The Supreme Kid*, starring Helen Shaver and Frank Moore. These two films were shot on location in British Columbia by local technicians in 16 mm (blown up to 35 mm for the theatres) and the processing was done in Vancouver. The nucleus of a film industry was forming.

In March 1973 the quota proposal was the subject of an Ontario Gallup poll: "It has been recommended by an official committee that all movie theatres be required to exhibit Canadian films for a total of eight weeks in every two years, in order to encourage the production of Canadian films. Would you approve, or disapprove, if such a law were introduced in the province?"

The idea was approved by 65 percent, with only 17 percent disapproving and 18 percent undecided. A majority in favour of Canadian features having their own screening time? But there was a follow-up question: "Some people say that although they approve this required use of Canadian movies in general, they themselves would not be particularly interested in going to see them. Do you feel this way or not?" Forty-seven percent said they were not interested, 37 percent were, and 16 percent had no opinion.

If the answer to the first part of the question had lifted our spirits, they were dashed by the answer to part two. Now we knew that English Canadians wanted a feature film industry and were willing to pay for it — as long as they could be excused from seeing the films. Could an industry that required mass support survive under these circumstances? The uncertainty did not discourage us from forging ahead.

CANADA TOASTS CANNES (1972–1974)

CHAPTER 9
AN ENGLISH CANADIAN HIT
1974

Photo : Lois Siegel.

Casting Richard Dreyfuss in *The Apprenticeship of Duddy Kravitz* was a coup: he had just come off his first starring role in *American Graffiti* and was about to become a household name in *Jaws*.

If there was ever a Canadian novel that could become a major motion picture it was Mordecai Richler's *The Apprenticeship of Duddy Kravitz*. The story of a Montreal Jewish boy longing to rise above his working-class roots and willing to go to any lengths to succeed had been a top-selling novel; surely it would do even better as a film. Producer John Kemeny recognized its potential early on and commissioned Canadian screenwriter Lionel Chetwynd to write a script. Kemeny was reasonably pleased with the first draft and sent it off to Richler for comment. Richler, who was living in England at the time, had worked as a screenwriter himself on several English features. He in turn passed the script to his good friend, director Ted Kotcheff, who suggested that if Richler would do a second draft, he would direct. This convergence of heavy hitters was just what was needed to put the picture on a fast track. The CFDC had already committed $300,000 and Montreal lawyer Gerald Schneider was set to raise the balance of the $650,000 needed to complete the picture.

The shoot in Montreal and the Laurentians created a lot of excitement. That Richard Dreyfuss was to play Duddy represented a casting coup — he had just come off his first starring role in George Lucas' *American Graffiti* and was about to become a household name in Steven Spielberg's *Jaws*. The role of Yvette, Duddy's girlfriend, went to Micheline Lanctôt, well known in Quebec for her starring role in Gilles Carle's *La vraie nature de Bernadette*. (My doctor, David Marcus, loved the novel and I had arranged for him to be an extra on the shoot in the Laurentians. During filming Richard Dreyfuss somehow cut his wrist on a shard of glass — and Marcus went from extra to saviour of the day.)

American films released in Canada came with a ready-made, large-scale promotional campaign complete with posters, trailers, stills, and media events. Nothing like that had ever been done for a

125

Canadian film, but we were determined to release *Duddy Kravitz* the American way (albeit without an American distributor). Harold Greenberg, president of the film's Canadian distributor, Astral Films, and his second-in-command, Mickey Stevenson, produced the trailers and posters and organized press conferences and premieres in every city across the country. Hopes were high; a box office hit in Canada would surely mean an even bigger hit in the U.S.

In the spring of 1974 *Duddy Kravitz* opened with a star-studded black-tie gala in Montreal. Gratien Gélinas introduced the attending dignitaries, among whom was our champion, Secretary of State Hugh Faulkner, and Harold Greenberg, rapidly becoming Canada's best-known moving pictures entrepreneur. The audience loved the film. One week later it had racked up an unprecedented $60,000 gross box office in Montreal's Place Ville Marie cinema and Toronto's Towne Cinema.

At long last, the CFDC could claim it had invested in an English-language hit. Stevenson estimated that the final returns in Canada alone would exceed $2 million. Since Canada represented 10 percent of the American market, this figure would undoubtedly translate tenfold when the film hit the States. An unheard-of twenty million! All we needed now was a major American distributor.

We knew we had to act fast. Arnold Kopelson of Inter-Ocean Films came on board to represent us. He arranged a series of special screenings for the majors in Los Angeles, all to take place in a week. Speed was essential; the rumour mill can work for or against you, and we didn't want to take any chances. Right after each screening Kopelson, Kemeny, and I would meet with their people and discuss the deal, laying great stress on the excellent figures in Canada. According to Kopelson, discussions in New York with Frank Yablans of Paramount got quite heated, culminating in Yablans yelling: "Don't you fuck with me!" But in the end, Paramount came through with the best offer: it wasn't the highest bid, but as the number one studio at the time it would create the most effective distribution campaign. And we were impressed that Paramount immediately entered the film in the Berlin film festival, where it won top prize, the Golden Bear.

Our excitement was short lived. Canada might represent 10 percent of the U.S. box office, but as we were about to learn, the U.S. was not automatically ten times the Canadian box office, especially if the U.S. distributor wasn't promoting the film as well as it would one of its own. We waited in vain for an encouraging word from Paramount.

Following the trail of *Duddy Kravitz* we had great expectations for four other pictures destined for the Canadian market in 1977 and based on Canadian stories. They all did well in Canada — *Who Has Seen the Wind* had a gross box office of $1.2 million, *Why Shoot the Teacher* $1.7 million, *Outrageous!* $700,000, and *Rabid* $800,000 — but generated little interest in the U.S.

With these five pictures we had come as close as we ever would to creating the feature film industry of which Nat Taylor and the interdepartmental committee had dreamed. We hadn't even realized that we had reached the peak — we were too disappointed by the view. Nevertheless, we had given a strong impetus to a production industry in the English language and we still believed that the federal and provincial governments had the courage to implement tough legislation for distribution.

Our 1972 cross-country trip to encourage the provinces to institute quotas and levies had put us in contact with a number of high-ranking officials. And so, to work more closely with them towards this end, we organized a national think tank on the future of Canadian cinema. Thanks to the Canada Council, we could offer the ideal location for this industry retreat: Stanley House, a former Governor General's residence surrounded by lawns, gardens, and ancient trees on the Gaspé peninsula.

Several provincial representatives agreed to meet with us. Among them were the executive assistant to the minister of B.C.'s

Industrial Development; the director of film and literary arts in Alberta's Department of Culture, Youth and Recreation; the director of promotion services in the Manitoba Department of Industry and Commerce; and Ontario's assistant deputy minister of Cultural Affairs in the Ministry of Colleges and Universities, as well as the director of services industries in the Department of Industry and Tourism. We were also joined by Peter Roberts, assistant to the Undersecretary of State; Peter Pearson, John Kemeny, and Martin Bochner from the film industry; and Penny Jacques of the Canada Council.

The results of the discussion, while mixed, were positive overall. Ontario was neutral about the prospect of quotas; Alberta was definitely against; and the Manitoba representative from the Department of Industry and Commerce was in favour. The B.C. representative could see the potential of a levy that would raise money from the theatres for homegrown production. The door, in other words, had not yet been shut.

It was a measure of the Corporation's continuing optimism that it was able to state unequivocally in its 1974–75 annual report: "Quotas and levies may still be some way off, but it seems clear that Canadian cinemas will soon start co-operating with Canadian producers in order to provide entertaining films for their audiences."

It wasn't until the late 1980s that I discovered the extent to which the dark forces arrayed against us had pre-empted the high ground. As a consultant for the secretary of state in 1986 I had access to some confidential departmental documents, and I learned that throughout the early 70s the CMPDA had been taking its complaints directly to the minister, completely bypassing the advisory group of which it was a member. Nor did we have the slightest idea that it was informing Jack Valenti and the MPAA of what was going on. The CMPDA's brief to the minister also confirmed the MPAA's thinly veiled contempt for the CFDC. Nothing, I realized, had changed since we met the majors at the interdepartmental

AN ENGLISH CANADIAN HIT (1974)

committee stage. The document was relentless in its condemnation of the CFDC:

> The absence of any meaningful influence from the ranks of experienced Canadian exhibition and distribution personnel on the decision-making activities of the CFDC has created a climate of naiveté, incompetence, bias and lack of judgment. CFDC-subsidized films have, in a number of cases, ludicrously low box office receipts. In other cases CFDC-sponsored product has been rejected by the CBC for TV on the basis of complete lack of acceptable quality. On the other hand, films like *Black Christmas* and *Duddy Kravitz* are two examples of sound commercial successes without the influence of legislation and less than a 25 percent support from the CFDC. Why did they succeed without Government intervention and only minority participation by the CFDC?
>
> A weak and willing Government in support of special interest groups can install a quota system but this Government cannot and will not compel the tax-payer to the box-office. Quotas in most other countries have been directly related to the necessary support of specific language needs and requirements within that country.

After all these years it hardly seems worthwhile to refute the various points in the CMPDA brief. After all, it provides only another link in the sorry chain that started back in 1909 when the U.S. consul in Winnipeg declared: "In this new country where all forms of amusement are scarce, moving pictures are welcomed, and there is no reason why the manufacturers of the United States should not control the business."

The Cabinet memorandum that had originally authorized the legislation to create the CFDC had stipulated that the Corporation's economic and cultural viability would be determined after five years of operations, and that time had arrived. The Treasury Board planned an in-depth study of the industry to determine what the CFDC had contributed to it. That's not what we wanted. We believed the memo had called for a study of the CFDC itself — how well or badly it worked on its own terms. Our own version could be completed quickly, and we needed decisions on our future. But we had no choice: the Treasury Board's study of the entire industry would take at least a year, during which it would have an excuse for not providing us with funds.

The Treasury Board assigned the task to Mr. Parikh, an officer at the Bureau of Management Consulting in the Department of Supply and Services. He called for making a clearer demarcation between unprofitable projects that had artistic merit and projects that brought in the money, artistic merit or no. "Mr. Parikh mistakenly assumes," I observed at the time, "that there is a clearly definable difference between cultural and commercial." Treasury disagreed; further delays ensued. Meanwhile, we were running out of our second $10 million.

Word quickly reached the industry that the CFDC's coffers were about to run dry. As ever, the Council of Canadian Filmmakers was very much on our side. Council members Kirwan Cox, Sandra Gathercole, and Peter Pearson created a lot of noise and pointed out that, if the collapse of the Canadian film industry hadn't already happened, it was imminent. In April 1974, Pearson, then chairman of the Council, delivered an impassioned speech to the Parliamentary Committee on Broadcasting, Films, and Assistance to the Arts:

> We commend the government for its bold concept in taking Canada into the feature film industry. The taxpayers have committed $20 million in expectation of seeing Canadian films for the first time in their neighbourhood theatres. These films have seldom appeared. In six years we have learned that the system does not work for Canadians. The film financing system does not work. Thirteen major features were produced in English Canada in 1972. Six in 1973. Only one in 1974 (to date). The film distribution system does not work. In 1972 less than 2 percent of the movies shown in Ontario were Canadian, less than 5 percent in Quebec — the supposed bedrock of Canadian cinema. The film exhibition system does not work. The foreign-dominated theatre industry, grossing over $140 million at the box office in 1972, is recycling only nickels and dimes into future domestic production. Clearly something is wrong. It is no wonder then that the Canadian Film Development Corporation cannot possibly work and neither can we.

AN ENGLISH CANADIAN HIT (1974)

Hugh Faulkner, who was keeping me informed of the ongoing discussions with the Treasury Board (I wasn't allowed to be present), told me of the Board's dissatisfaction with the CFDC's investment in films that attacked the government. He was referring specifically to Michel Brault's *Les ordres*, a powerful, documentary-style indictment of the martial law imposed in Quebec in 1970 after the FLQ's kidnapping of the British Consul in Montreal. But the CFDC wasn't alone in financing such films; the CBC was also pursuing an independent line, claiming that its mandate called for it to be objective on political matters even though the government itself financed it. No doubt it was confusion about the meaning and application of the arms-length principle that contributed to the Treasury Board's inability to make up its mind about the CFDC's future.

No matter what the government thought of it, Pierre David was convinced that he could make a lot of money with *Les ordres*. The film, which debuted in Quebec theatres in 1974, brought home the Best Director award for Brault from the 1975 Cannes film festival competition. But to David's dismay, this did not lead to significant international sales:"It became very clear to me at one point that the language was an insurmountable barrier. Everywhere. I couldn't generate foreign sales. Despite all the help — the festivals, the CFDC, the Quebec government — you can't make people go to the theatre."

Ironically, more than twenty years later, in 1997, *Les ordres* was commemorated with an official Canadian postage stamp.

Sweet Movie, a 1974 Canada/France co-production starring Carole Laure as a victimized beauty who descends into madness, served as another example of the questions that a controversial film could raise in the House of Commons. *Maclean's* magazine had warned its readers:

> Beware *Sweet Movie*. Yugoslavian director Dusan Makavejev shares the same credo as Ken Russell — nothing succeeds like excess. But Makavejev at least (it's a small plus) has the courage of his perversions. (I counted eight on-camera acts of vomiting, five of urination,

131

four of defecation)... Some people may be mad that a movie with such ingredients was made and mad as hell that the CFDC has a $115,000 investment in it.

Members of the House responded in kind:

> Question No. 2879
> Did the CFDC fund the film *Sweet Movie* as reported in *Maclean's* magazine?
> Does the government consider that financial support for pornographic movies is a proper use of public money?

For a cultural bureaucrat, it was all part of a day's work. I had to write a detailed memorandum to the minister justifying the CFDC's investment so that he in turn could answer the questions in the House. In the memo I pointed out Makavejev's outstanding international reputation (supported by quotes from such reputable film publications as *Film Quarterly*) and what that meant for a France/Canada co-production on the global festival circuit; the track record of the co-producing partners (Montreal's Michael Costom and brothers Vincent and Louis Malle from Paris); and the Canadian content of the film itself. And of course I mentioned how important it was to the budding career of Canadian actress Carole Laure.

The kerfuffle didn't seem to interfere in any way with the distribution of the film; on the contrary, it stirred the journalists. Les Wedman, our sternest West Coast critic, wrote in *The Vancouver Sun*: "Aside from the love scenes and murder in a vat of sugar and Carole Laure's death in a bath of melting chocolate, *Sweet Movie* is an extraordinary work of artistic merit without inhibition, directed by one of the most serious and lucid filmmakers on the international scene." I'm pretty sure Wedman never mentioned that the CFDC had invested in the picture.

The Treasury Board, meanwhile, continued its reflections on the Corporation's future. It had received its report from the Bureau of Management Consulting but had not decided to renew our appropriation. I was upset at Treasury's complaint that the CFDC wasn't making enough money from its investments. According to the Treasury, we weren't fulfilling the optimistic forecasts of the interdepartmental committee that the feature film industry in Canada would be a thriving business; we should, they felt, be able to return much more than 30 percent of our investments. We were neatly sandwiched — by now a familiar sensation — between the Treasury Board and our clients, who weren't making enough money to plough back into the industry.

We finally did get a green light for a third appropriation of $5 million, which arrived only in the following, 1976 fiscal year— by which time it had been further reduced to $3,433,000. Expecting another $10 million, the amount came as an insulting setback. But as it turned out, this marked the first of what was to become the Corporation's regular annual appropriation. Permanent funding at last!

Even with the relative successes of *Kamouraska* (which ran for fifteen weeks in Washington) and *The Apprenticeship of Duddy Kravitz*, the total theatrical revenue of CFDC-financed films had levelled off at about $800,000 to $900,000 a year — not enough to fund an industry. Canadian feature films, it was clear, would have to depend on the continuing support of the federal and provincial governments.

By 1975 we had about seventy-five titles that were returning money. Nine of these had paid us back more than $50,000 each; these included *Deux femmes en or* and *L'initiation,* as well as *The Apprenticeship of Duddy Kravitz,* which by then had returned $334,888. A further sixty-four titles were paying some money back but were not yet in profit, and might never be. Fifty-six titles in release hadn't yet returned anything to the Corporation, including *Fortune and Men's Eyes, Lies My Father Told Me,* and *A Fan's Notes.* Even today, most of the features that have returned profits to the Corporation were produced in the early years.

Meanwhile, in the totally different world of Quebec, producers of feature films continued to make good use of CFDC funds.

Gratien Gélinas and I would sit in the Montreal boardroom and listen to all kinds of proposals. Pierre Lamy was particularly adept in thinking up imaginative schemes to get the maximum contribution from the Corporation, no matter how often we told him they were unacceptable. Not far behind were Marie-Josée Raymond and Claude Fournier, as well as Denis and Claude Héroux.

Negotiating was the one aspect of my role as executive director that I most relished. I often wondered what was in my genes that made me so keen on getting a good return on the government's money. Perhaps it was the influence of Nat Taylor and his conviction that making features was a profitable business. If it *was* profitable, why shouldn't the government's money be treated the same as anybody else's? In the early days I'd learned a simple formula. All money invested in a project is recovered *pro rata* and *pari passu*: as it is put in, so is it taken out. Once the original investment is recovered, the producer gets half of the profits and the investors get the other half. Most of our clients, however, wanted us to accept less so that they could get more. "After all, there's a difference between our money and the government's," they would say. To which I invariably countered, "Why should there be a difference?" I remember negotiating with André Link about the profits of *L'initiation* in a restaurant on the Via Veneto in Rome. We were always arguing about the CFDC's percentage of profits. Link and his partner John Dunning made pictures that challenged the boundaries of acceptability, but they were making money from the spunk and sex appeal of their films, so why shouldn't we get our share? Our meetings inevitably ended with both of us thinking we should have gotten more.

I also admired them for their ability to discover and finance rebellious artistic filmmakers, not the least of whom was David Cronenberg and his script called *Orgy of the Blood Parasites* (a.k.a. 1975's *Shivers* or *The Parasite Murders*). We knew from the title that this would be a risky project. There would likely be questions in the House of Commons, but we hoped it would be a profitable artistic investment.

Now one of the world's most renowned cult filmmakers, Cronenberg says he liked working with the Montreal producers in 1975 precisely because "they were businessmen. They didn't care about the censors. And they were businessmen who thought scandals were great because it got free attention for movies. When *Shivers* was 'the big subject' in the House of Commons, I thought 'God, don't they have anything better to do?' But John and André loved it." Ted Rouse of the CFDC's Toronto office recalls the flak that Cronenberg took when the film first came out: "He was living in a rooming house down in Kensington Market and his landlady had just read the review. She was so angry with him, she kicked him out. 'That's it. You're not going to live in this house any more!' she said."

Cronenberg swore recently that a 1975 article about *Shivers* written by Robert Fulford (published under the pseudonym Marshall Delaney) in *Saturday Night* magazine "probably took a year or two off my working life." Fulford's piece was scathing, not only about Cronenberg's work, but the CFDC's very existence:

> If using public money to produce films like *The Parasite Murders* is the only way that English Canada can have a film industry, then perhaps English Canada should not have a film industry. One should say it straight out: *The Parasite Murders*, written and directed by David Cronenberg and produced by Ivan Reitman, with $70,000 of the Canadian taxpayers' money, is an atrocity, a disgrace to everyone connected with it — including the taxpayers. The question it raises is an old one now, but *The Parasite Murders* brings it to life again: should we subsidize junk (or worse than junk) in order to create an "industry" that will also possibly produce indigenous and valuable feature films?

One man's junk, evidently, is another man's entertainment. If Fulford hoped his negative criticism would keep the public away, he was wrong. *Shivers* paid back the CFDC, as have all of Cronenberg's other films to date. But at the time, the article was a thorny issue for the CFDC. The censors had approved the picture, but the minister was nonetheless concerned about repercussions from Fulford's article in Cabinet and the Treasury Board.

135

"I don't think the government would have even noticed if it hadn't been for that article, frankly," said Cronenberg. "First of all, I think it was one of the first movies that ever made the CFDC back some money [it wasn't]; I don't think the government cared until they were forced to care."

Scandal may have intimidated the government, but it often served as free advertising that brought Canadian films to the attention of the movie-going audience. While I was busy writing memos for the minister to defend the CFDC's investments in films of questionable content, an enthusiastic young producer named Robert Lantos was in search of it. Pity he didn't ask us to invest in his first feature, Gilles Carle's *L'ange et la femme* (1977), a dreamlike black and white movie about a love affair with the angel Gabriel, starring Carole Laure and Lewis Furey.

"We were all counting on big box office because Carole was the number one star in Quebec at the time and she was going to do very, very scandalous and sexy things with Lewis on camera. It was supposed to cause a scandal and it caused no stir at all," laughed Lantos, now Chairman and CEO of Serendipity Point Films.

Had we financed it, however, the nude scenes would have undoubtedly raised eyebrows, but Lantos had never heard of the CFDC at the time:

> The idea for it was born in a nightclub in Montreal called Night Magic, where I became friendly with Carole and Gilles. Nobody was working and no films were being made, and she said: "How about making this really small movie that Gilles wants to make?" There was a ten-page outline and I read it: it was kind of lyrical, poetic, black and white . . . a very small movie. Because I had never produced a film before, they said they would all do it for free. Gilles would get a crew for free and I would produce it, but it would have to be shot in January. It was the only window.

After Lantos made a quick phone call introducing himself to George Destounis of Famous and mentioning Carle's and Laure's involvement, "Destounis said: 'I only have $30,000 left' and I said 'okay.'"

The scandal-free release in Quebec meant they didn't make back their total $65,000 budget in Canada. Capitalizing on an obscure international critic's prize in Europe, Lantos and Victor Loewy, his partner, sealed a distribution deal for France and Belgium. *L'ange et la femme* was soon hailed as a "masterpiece" in the reviews, and Lantos began to understand the importance of the European market and trade paper reviews.

The co-production treaties we had pioneered in 1965 had become a recognized means of financing Canadian films, and we continued to view co-production with European countries as an important way for Canada to break into the international market and simultaneously provide new sources of funding. And now we could boast of a new treaty: after many attempts, in 1975 we were finally able to sign an agreement with the U.K. Faulkner asked me to accompany him to London in September for the signing.

A Cabinet shuffle the next year would mark the end of Hugh Faulkner's tenure as secretary of state. In the *Time* and *Reader's Digest* affair he had led a cavalry charge in the face of enemy fire, and turned to find that he was almost alone. His battle for control of Canadian newspapers and magazines, like the battle for Canadian cinemas, had been lost. It must have been disheartening, but the struggle continues today. When the Liberals lost the election in '79, the man who had done the most for Canadian film as minister decided that his future lay elsewhere, and abandoned politics altogether.

CHAPTER 10
CHANGING OF THE GUARD
1976–1978

(Left to right) Producer Harry Gulkin, star Carole Laure and director Gilles Carle take a break on the set of *A Weekend in the Country* (1977).

J ohn Roberts, the next secretary of state, was determined to make his own contribution to the Canadian film industry: he intended not only to solve the CFDC's perpetual funding crisis but to find a solution for the nagging distribution problem. Roberts was a film buff, and we counted ourselves lucky to have a minister with some knowledge of the moving-picture milieu.

Soon after his appointment, I met Roberts to discuss our program forecast. The Corporation, I explained, had been badly served by the Treasury Board over the years. He immediately agreed to request an additional $1 million in supplementary estimates that year to replace the million we had been entitled to the previous fall but had not received. I also wanted to make sure we would get the last $1 million from the original $10 million. The Treasury Board had said it would be made available to us but later withdrew it without explanation. The Corporation's relatively small budget had been diminished without any cause or consultation, and Roberts agreed that he had grounds to get it back. After all, we had been trying to jump-start a major industry.

On the distribution front, Roberts also determined that quotas were not the way to go. The Corporation's efforts to introduce provincial quotas and levies during Faulkner's term had backfired when the CMPDA's counter-propaganda had convinced backbench MPs that any interference at the box office would taint the government's public image. Roberts thought there must be another way.

We continued that year to take an active role in promoting co-production treaties. In February 1977 Gratien Gélinas, producer David Perlmutter, our faithful lawyer Jo Beaubien, and I headed for Bonn to sign a preliminary agreement with the Federal Republic of Germany. Perlmutter recalls a rather odd incident that occurred during the meeting:

CHANGING OF THE GUARD (1976-1978)

141

Saturday morning we arrived at the German offices to officially sign the treaty and everybody was gathered around the table. The secretaries brought in all the documents, and we sat there and signed them. Then came the German sparkling wine — I hesitate to use the word champagne — and we all started toasting. At that moment the secretaries suddenly produced scissors, and without a word of warning, cut our ties off. "That's the custom in this area of Germany during Lent," they explained. "We're allowed to cut off the boss's tie." They just did it. We meekly submitted.

In 1977 Canada once again had the honour of having two films in the Official Competition at Cannes, both of which brought home prizes. Jean Beaudin's *J.A. Martin, photographe* is about a woman who, hoping to reinvigorate her fifteen-year marriage, joins her husband on his yearly trip around Quebec to take portrait photographs. Monique Mercure shared the best actress award for her performance with Shelley Duval for her role in Robert Altman's *Three Women. Auteur* filmmaker Jean-Pierre Lefevbre's *Le vieux pays ou Rimbaud est mort*, about the adventures of a Quebecer who goes to France to learn about his ancestors, garnered the Ecumenical Award honouring films for their humanitarian values. Lefevbre had directed 1969's *La chambre blanche*, one of the first films we had invested in. Although we had never received any returns on his films, they contributed to the reputation of the Canadian film industry. The late film critic Jay Scott considered him "Canada's most accomplished filmmaker."

As usual, the Riviera festival gave us an opportunity to exchange views with our co-production partners. This time I was holding tense discussions with British producers. Canadians weren't being given significant roles either behind or in front of the camera. Co-production treaties, it transpired, didn't necessarily work in favour of Canadian producers hoping to tell Canadian stories. I maintained that we would interpret the treaty to get as many Canadians in creative roles as possible, a position to which the Brits were very much opposed. The object of the exercise, in their view, was to produce popular films, and bureaucrats should not get in the way.

"Producers like you and your Canadian counterparts are attractive to financiers looking for tax shelters," I retorted, "because of big budgets and presumed international potential. The way you're structuring your deals doesn't do much to develop a Canadian film industry."

This was certainly true of the two Italian/Canadian films in the works at the time. Both were Italian stories: *Night of the High Tide* with Canadian producers Marie-José Raymond and Claude Fournier (who had also worked on the script) and *A Special Day*, written and directed by Ettore Scola and starring Sophia Loren and Marcello Mastroianni. The film, which featured the then well-known Canadian actors Françoise Berd and John Vernon, was shot in a Montreal studio and involved a significant Canadian crew. We had agreed to invest in *A Special Day* because we were keen to get Loren and Mastroianni working in Canada and because Carlo Ponti, the producer, had talked about doing a second film based on a Canadian story. The second film was never made but thirty years later Carlo Ponti Jr. directed an Italian/Canadian co-production, *Between Strangers*, starring his mother Sophia Loren and shot in Canada. Montreal is a great location, but a Canadian story was still nowhere in sight.

The 100 percent capital cost allowance (CCA) officially introduced in 1975 had by now given renewed impetus to the production of feature films in Canada. The Corporation's 1976–77 annual report listed thirteen features that had been produced that fiscal year using the CCA but not requesting any financial aid from the CFDC. Since its first year of existence, the Corporation had known that it could succeed in creating an industry only if a significant number of films were made without its investment. Such films should be encouraged and applauded, I thought, because they lessened pressure on CFDC resources and expanded the financial base of the industry. That's why we wanted to compliment the producers by mentioning the titles in our annual report. Among them were *Jacob Two-Two Meets the Hooded Fang*, based on the children's book

143

by Mordecai Richler and produced by Harry Gulkin, and *Welcome to Blood City*, starring Jack Palance and Keir Dullea, produced by Marilyn Stonehouse, and photographed by Reginald Morris —a seventy–thirty Canada/U.K. co-production. André Link and John Dunning's contribution had the snazzy title *Ilsa: The Tigress of Siberia*.

The fall of 1977 saw the shooting of Robert Lantos's *In Praise of Older Women*, starring Tom Berenger and Helen Shaver in a story of a young Hungarian's weakness for older women. Although I usually had doubts about financing any first feature from new producers, we were encouraged by the popularity of Steven Vizinczey's novel and by the fact that Robert had produced *L'ange et la femme* on a small budget.

Lantos told us an interesting story about how he and his colleague Stephen J. Roth got the rights to *In Praise of Older Women*:

> During my first encounter with Steven Vizinczey in a restaurant in London, he said that his book was not for sale; it never would be, and no one would ever make a movie of it. He only met me because I had the producer credit from *L'ange et la femme*. At our next meeting, we were sitting in his study and he challenged Stephen to a chess game. As it happened, there was a chessboard right there. Roth saw it and asked him: "Are you any good?" And Steven said: "Well, I'm very good, I'm very, very good, do you want to play?" So they played, and Roth beat him. Vizinczey swallowed his pride sold us the rights on the spot.

Just days before shooting was to begin, the lead actress pulled out. I was not, however, about to let this one slip through our hands. As Lantos tells it:

> I was at the closing at the CFDC offices. Michael was in the room, with a couple of lawyers and Harold Greenberg. "We have a big problem," Harold said. "Our star has just quit. We can't sign the contract without an actress." Michael replied: "Sure we can. Let's sign anyway. You can easily get another actress before shooting begins."

S. Wayne Clarkson and Bill Marshall chose the film to close Toronto's 1978 Festival of Festivals, as it was then called. The Ontario censor board had made cuts to the film, and Lantos had wisely turned that into a publicity coup. The story was all over the Toronto papers; on opening night the theatre was mobbed and a second screening had to be added. "There were two packed houses: it was madness," Lantos beamed. Two copies of the film were in the projection booth — one censored and the other uncensored. Who knows which version the audience saw that night?

One day that winter, out of the clear blue sky, Jo Beaubien tipped me off about a top-secret rumour. Beaubien, who had his own sources of information on the French "old boy net" in Ottawa, had heard that Michael McCabe, the assistant deputy minister of Consumer and Corporate Affairs, was going to replace me as head of the CFDC. "This can't be serious," I figured, although I did remember a brief conversation about my future with André Fortier, the deputy secretary of state. I barely gave it a second thought.

In early 1978 John Roberts made an announcement on film policy that drew applause from the Canadian production industry. His speech to the House of Commons began with an eloquent testimony of the current state of affairs:

> The feature film industry is young. It is seriously under-financed and regarded as high risk by investors, banks, and other lending institutions. It is struggling to cope with foreign domination and to compete in Canada at prices that the Canadian filmmaker has difficulty in matching. It has not yet acquired the business acumen and management expertise of its foreign competitors. It has the task of trying to instill a Canadian spirit or character into its films without at the same time risking their universal appeal. It is trying to counterbalance a deeply ingrained preference of Canadians for American and other foreign films.

This was just what we wanted to hear. Roberts, we hoped, would be the first minister able to align Canada with other countries that had imposed financial and legislative controls on foreign cinema. His officials had begun work on a proposal to impose a

145

special tax on foreign distributors in Canada. Since the change in the Excise Tax Act would come under the jurisdiction of the Department of Finance, its officials would have to be actively involved in the drafting of the formal request to Cabinet.

The policy had been neither finalized nor approved when Roberts went on to announce it:

> I have raised with my colleagues in government the possibility, if all else fails, of placing a special Excise Tax on the profits of distributors. I have also discussed the matter with the distributors themselves and with Jack Valenti. If the major distributors decline my invitation to participate voluntarily in the development of our industry, I shall press ahead with a special Excise tax. My instructions are that the door remains open: obviously we would rather not close it.

The minister forgot the instructions; he tried to play hardball and failed. Roberts didn't seem to realize that the Department of Finance — although it was part of the same Trudeau government — wasn't playing on his team. It was, for all intents and purposes, on the side of hard-nosed lobbyist Jack Valenti, a man whose political savvy has blinded most of his opponents. Finance officials reckoned that any such Excise Tax Act scheme was going to end up costing the taxpayers money, and they didn't believe it was something the voting public wanted to pay for anyway. Roberts had completely underestimated the powerful lobbying force of Valenti and his highly effective Canadian minion, Millard Roth. He didn't know what he was up against and his proposal got shot down in flames. "All I can remember is the bloody Finance officials who kept saying that this has bad public appeal, to have a tax," Roberts said recently.

John Roberts should have had his Excise Act change in place before he spoke. When the Department of Finance landed on the same side as the theatre owners and the MPAA, he was left with the old position of moral suasion. Roberts made a trip to Los Angeles to beseech Jack Valenti and the studio heads, but with painfully predictable results. The late George Heiber, then president of the CMPDA, summed it up: "I am pleased at this moment with the film policy statement. I think it is very fair. There were no limitations put on it; we're not putting any on the government and they are not putting any on us."

His film policy in shambles, it would seem a good time for Roberts to lie low, rethink his strategy, and consult his experts. Then again, perhaps he didn't have any trusted strategists to advise him at least to stay away from the front line. Surprisingly, he set himself up again.

On March 3, 1978, *Toronto Star* columnist Sid Adilman — who had close ties to the Liberal party — delivered the scoop: "Movie man Spencer about to be dropped." Adilman pegged Roberts as a man oblivious to what was happening around him. "John Roberts is poised to drop a bombshell on Canada's movie-making field. He's ready to drop Michael Spencer, executive director of the Canadian Film Development Corp. for 10 years, and replace him with Ottawa mandarin Michael McCabe . . . who has no movie world experience." At first this article took me by surprise: I had talked informally about my future with the undersecretary of state, but I had absolutely no official warning that things had gone this far.

The Adilman scoop had, as it turned out, gauged the industry reaction perfectly. "This is an insult," said one movie source. "Just when Canada's movie industry is taking off with several winners, we get a guy who, no matter how talented in other fields, knows nothing about how the industry works. This is just a rank political appointment, straight and simple, and it's disgusting Roberts would do that."

Harold Greenberg had invited my wife, Maqbool, and me to join him in his limousine for the trip from Montreal to Rideau Hall where the Governor General had organized a special screening of *J.A. Martin, photographe* for the members of the film industry. Harold and I certainly had many things to talk about. Neither of us had seen the Toronto papers that day, but he had heard rumours and asked me if I was going to resign. (I recall saying, "Yes, but . . .")

Once we had arrived and were searching for our seats Maqbool was surprised to suddenly find herself face to face with the Prime

Minister. "Oh! Trudeau!" she exclaimed. After I stepped in to make formal introductions she made quite an impression, not only because of the striking sari she wore. "You're the greatest thing to happen to Canada," she told him. He swiftly replied, "What about Mr. Spencer?" "Mr. Spencer happened to me," she said: "You happened to Canada."

At the dinner afterwards, Mr. Trudeau was greeting guests with the Governor General when Maqbool was once again presented to him. "Namasthe," he said to her, placing his hands together in traditional Hindu greeting.

"Mr. Prime Minister," I whispered, "Maqbool is a Muslim."

Without a moment's hesitation, Trudeau said "Salaam alaikam" and raised his hand before his face in Muslim salutation. Maqbool was much impressed by his speedy riposte. I was equally impressed by his 1960 Mercedes 300SL sport coupe in which he zoomed off towards his Sussex Drive residence.

Back in the "real" world, *Maclean's* magazine headline writers went skimming in shallow waters and came up with "new proof that nice guys finished last." Journalist Kaspars Dzeguze slammed Roberts with a shocking observation from one of his own staff members: "He's packed into his first 18 months as Secretary of State as much bungling as took previous secretaries years to achieve."

The journalist continued: "Roberts has now outdone himself with the callous way he's engineered the dismissal of Michael Spencer, 58, founding executive director of the Canadian Film Development Corporation, in order to replace him with a master of the Ottawa power game, Michael McCabe, 40."

Looking through all the old news clippings from that period made me realize how much the industry supported me and how much egg the minister had on his face. But I guess I knew I ought to leave after ten years, and I was starting to think about the direction my career should take next.

I didn't agree with Ottawa's choice of a replacement who had no knowledge of the industry. I had come to the position of executive director on the basis of an industry consensus that I was the best person for the job. Everybody was in on the act. At least a dozen people were interviewed for the job while I was running the Corporation. When I was finally given the role, I had a feeling that it was with the full consent of the government and the Canadian film industry, and that Gérard Pelletier had the clout to impose this choice on the Privy Council.

But now the Privy Council Office was listening to another drummer altogether, and I was summoned to Ottawa to discuss the termination of my appointment. At that time Michael Pitfield was the Clerk of the Privy Council. John Roberts recalled the situation:

> Michael Pitfield had come back from a stint at the Harvard Business School on governance. So the government adopted this idea that management was a science. And if you could manage one thing, if you were a properly trained manager you could manage anything. So not only did the government decide that we should move ministers around every two or three years, which was a bad idea, but they decided that we should move civil servants around. So I suspect, if we can use the word *victim* in relation to what happened to you, that you were a victim of the Harvard Business School approach to business management.

The idea was that any deputy minister could be freely transferred from one general area of responsibility to another. A deputy minister of Finance could easily become the deputy minister of Fisheries. But could an assistant deputy minister of Consumer and Corporate Affairs become an effective executive director of the CFDC? The clients of the CFDC and the film industry didn't think so. They believed that some expertise of film production and distribution would be a requisite.

One way or another, my term as executive director was over. But I still had one more co-production treaty to initial. John Roberts felt that he could win strong support from the influential Jewish community in his Toronto riding if he were to sign a co-production treaty with Israel. A lack of film ideas isn't a handicap to negotiating a co-production treaty; indeed, many have been signed long before any films have been produced under them. And the fact that Canada had already made one film with Israel gave the officials in Roberts's office and in his riding a good enough reason to request a treaty.

The two governments quickly agreed to meet in Tel Aviv. Politically, it seemed a good idea for Roberts to be part of the Canadian delegation, along with Pete Legault from the CFDC office in Montreal and me. (I didn't anticipate any awkwardness with Roberts during the trip, and none occurred. He didn't raise the matter of my departure and neither did I.)

Aside from the treaty, the highlight of the trip was visiting the Dead Sea, where I observed a rare bird, the Dead Sea Sparrow. (Legault was more curious about the legendary sea, and jumped in fully clothed to see if he would float. Luckily, he did.) And since it was an official visit, we were given a tour of the military headquarters on the Golan Heights. I tried to look interested as we were briefed on the tactics of international peacekeeping, but really I was much more intrigued by the migrating storks I had seen on our way up to the Heights.

The Canada/Israel treaty would be the last one I would negotiate. Nonetheless, in my last few months at the CFDC I travelled as much as possible, including my last trip to the Cannes film festival as executive director. (We didn't have a feature film in competition that year, but I did a lot schmoozing at the parties.)

On June 1, 1978, Michael McCabe became the second executive director of the Canadian Film Development Corporation, and hired me as a consultant for three months.

In the end, with a combination of luck and good judgment, my retirement from the CFDC worked to my advantage. It was clear that the industry was very much on my side. I felt appreciated and supported by my peers. In a way, I had turned the tables on the bureaucracy; they had expected to quietly nudge me into the shadows, and instead had been faced with a barrage of bad publicity.

If anyone came out of that situation looking foolish, it certainly wasn't me.

A roast was given in my honour at the Grand Ballroom of the Sheraton Centre in Toronto in June 1978. It was a super party, a long evening with many speakers. (Much wine flowed, which no doubt contributed to the length of the speeches.) Royce Frith as master of ceremonies opened the proceedings with "First off, ladies and gentlemen, I want to state a basic principle that is called the 'time' rule. Everyone is expected to limit themselves in this roasting to five minutes or so." Knowing the prolixity of my colleagues in the business and the quantity of wine available, I wished him good luck.

Martin Bochner set the tone of the evening:

> I look back at these ten years of the CFDC and I wonder why this man gets anything. Think of all the people in the industry, in this room, giants of the industry, who never got a dinner. Harold Greenberg, for instance, who in the last four years has had ninety-three cocktail parties and press conferences to announce the production of more pictures than have been released by 20th Century Fox, Universal, and Columbia — and made three of them. He never got a dinner.
>
> But this man, what's-his-name, he gets a dinner. I'll tell you why. He gets a dinner because of that indefinable finesse that turned "Definitely, yes, we'll do it" into "Maybe," "Maybe," into "No," and "No" into "Participation up to two hundred and fifty thousand dollars after you re-write, re-cast, and re-finance?"
>
> And finally, he gets a dinner because he's a hell of a nice guy who after ten years of a thankless job and a position where everybody in this world took potshots at him, if he had to do it all over again, he might just try it.

Denis Héroux, who was known for his sardonic sense of humour, said, "When I met you the first time ten years ago, you looked like a Scottish Methodist minister — not likely to put money into porno pictures. This Brit will never succeed in dealing with French Canadians." Denis looked at me sidelong to judge how his remarks were going over. "You still look like a Methodist minister," he said, "but last week the Quebec Producers Association at their annual meeting gave you a standing ovation."

151

Donald Brittain and Bill Carrick, two friends from my previous life and now sadly deceased, showed up at the roast. Brittain was and still is Canada's best known international documentary filmmaker (*Memorandum*, *Volcano: An Inquiry Into the Life and Death of Malcolm Lowry*, *Bethune: The Making of a Hero*). He must have been considering switching from documentary to fiction: "Spencer never let our friendship stand in the way of screwing up my career and I'm delighted as hell that he's getting out of the business."

Bill Carrick was a genius in another category: wildlife photography. We had worked together on a documentary entitled *World in a Marsh* in the 1950s and had kept in touch ever since, connected by our mutual interest in birds. Carrick was working on the wind tunnel in which Budge Crawley had hoped to shoot part of his last feature film, *The Strange One*, when he fell to his death in 2002.

Budge Crawley was the only roaster who had met my father. He remembered him as a proper English gentleman who had given me good advice as a child: "When travelling abroad, speak English, and if they don't understand, speak it louder and slower."

Next up was George Destounis, who expressed his disdain for Royce's "time rule." "I get five minutes to express ten years of frustration!?" he said. Then it was just one zinger after another.

"You've heard he's a bird-watcher, and there are many interpretations of that."

"We had a lunch date. He shows up in the god-damnedest outfit, with a scarf around his neck, so I dubbed him Darryl Zanuck."

". . . A good, safe journey, Michael, good luck, and a particularly long stay in Bombay."

Finally, Gordon Pinsent: "And they call themselves friends of yours, Michael. I imagine you're relieved to see a real friend stand up here now. A simple, honest, hard-working, deep-sea fisherman–type actor who has no axe to grind."

Then it was my turn to grind my axe. "George, if you could read scripts as well as you play blackjack, we'd all be rich."

"Young directors won't have any trouble getting money from the CFDC if they're under thirty and female," I said, eyeing Michael McCabe.

"When I was making only twenty bucks a week, I asked Budge Crawley for a raise and he gave me the classic response: Do you want to make money or make films?"

There was one legendary story about George Destounis I was happy to share with the party-goers at the Sheraton that evening. "I'll always remember this particular moment with George. There he was, gazing with amazement at the terrace of the Carleton Hotel in Cannes where a hundred producers and distributors were making deals over champagne and café au lait. 'It's the largest amount of money I ever heard of in my life,' he paused for dramatic effect, 'that never changed hands.'"

When it was all over, Ted Rouse presented me with a leather-bound, gold-plated book containing signatures and remarks from my distinguished colleagues, which included my highly esteemed mentor, Guy Roberge. Sitting there on the dais, I looked around the room and thought, "I must have done something right."

"Mildly Roasted, Not Burned" (*Variety*, June 28, 1978), I set off with my wife to drive from Bremerhaven, Germany, to Bombay, India, in my own Mercedes.

CHANGING OF THE GUARD (1976-1978)

CHAPTER 11
100 PERCENT TAX SHELTER ABUSE
1978–1979

"The cumulative effect of all those lousy films had not yet been felt on the industry as a whole," author Michael Spencer notes in this chapter.

I returned from the heat of Bombay anxious to get back into the industry and a cooler climate. I really wanted to be a producer, and Pierre Lamy provided me with the opportunity — we formed a company called Lamy, Spencer and Associates and started looking for projects to produce.

Under the Privy Council's conflict of interest rules at the time I had to wait six months before making an application for funding to the CFDC, but we eventually received a green light for *Les beaux souvenirs*, a psychological drama of despair and suicide directed by Francis Mankiewicz. We were certain we had a recipe for success: Mankiewicz's previous film, *Les bons débarras*, had been very popular in Quebec and we had the same scriptwriter on this one, the reclusive Réjean Ducharme. Lamy had made a deal to co-produce with the NFB, which would be responsible for half the production cost and would assign a producer of its own. Lamy was still the take-charge guy I had relied on when I was at the CFDC. He thought I should concentrate on raising money while he did the actual producing. The picture turned out to be a disappointment, certainly not one of Mankiewicz's *chef-d'oeuvres*.

The year 1978 was marked by a sudden proliferation of Canadian movies. The impetus for this outpouring, however, was strictly financial: by this time the potential for tax-free investments in Canadian films — a direct result of the 100 percent capital cost allowance (CCA) introduced back in 1975 to give them an advantage over foreign productions — had become widely known in the investment community.

Compared with the twenty or so features made with CFDC assistance in the early 1970s, the authoritative Canadian feature film index lists seventy-two features in production in 1978; eighty-two in 1979; seventy-five in 1980, and fifty-seven in 1981. All these films (with the exception of the four or five produced by the NFB every year) would have benefited from the 100 percent write-off.

Canadian investors were bewitched by the prospect of making money in show business, especially when such big names as Richard Burton and John Cassavetes were involved. Doctors and dentists in particular were sheltering their incomes in this way. After a year or two, though, they realized that lawyers and accountants were getting most of the money, and that despite the tax relief other investments were more likely to be profitable than Canadian feature films.

In their 1996 book *Mondo Canuck*, Geoff Pevere and Greig Dymond have this to say about the films produced during the tax-shelter 70s:

> As much as one might be inclined to bury the period's memory, in much the same manner that the period buried the movies it produced, the national folly that was Hollywood North cannot be forgotten and for these reasons. First, because it reveals much about the inevitable schizophrenia that grips a country trying to produce commercial culture according to bureaucratic blueprints; second, because it stands as a particularly abject example of what tends to happen when Canadians attempt to be just like Americans, except without the history, money, population, promotional savvy or market base; and third because it is a national farce of truly riveting dimensions.

At the time, I didn't feel dismayed by the sorry quality of the films that resulted from the tax break. The cumulative effect of all those lousy films had not yet been felt on the industry as a whole; as well, sometimes years pass between the production of a film and its eventual release. And, not wanting I suppose to throw the baby out with the bathwater, *Mondo Canuck* even recommends Daryl Duke's 1978 *Silent Partner*, starring Elliott Gould as a bank teller who outsmarts a thief, and Louis Malle's 1980 *Atlantic City*, about a croupier who dreams of going to Monte Carlo, an eighty–twenty Canada/France co-production produced by Denis Héroux, John Kemeny, and Jo Beaubien, who had graduated to executive producer.

The CFDC invested in eighty-two of the tax-shelter films made in 1978 through 1981. Among them was *Meatballs*, the wildly successful slapstick comedy about a second-rate summer camp directed by Ivan Reitman and produced by John Dunning and André Link. I was proud to sit in the audience for the premiere in Toronto, since I had started the ball rolling on this film before leaving for India. The Corporation invested $200,000 in *Meatballs* and continues to receive returns on it. The producers had even taken the precaution of getting a U.S. distributor lined up before the film was shot, so as to avoid the problems that *Duddy Kravitz* had encountered.

Meatballs was a winner among the tax-shelter films, but there were plenty of losers. *Mr. Patman* (1980), for example, about a man working at a psychiatric hospital who starts to lose his mind, was directed by the U.K.'s John Guillermin, written by Canadian Thomas J. Hedley, and starred James Coburn along with Canadian actress Kate Nelligan. It obtained a CFDC investment of $500,000 on a budget of $6,900,000, a long way over the $200,000 ceiling we were still maintaining when I left the Corporation. The film never got a theatrical release, finishing up on CBC-TV — a dead loss for the investors.

Other Canadian features during this period had memorable titles, if not memorable content: *Big Meat Eater (The Butcher of Burquitlam)*, *Hog Wild*, *Mondo Strip*, and *Some Do It for Money Some Do It for Fun*. Harold Greenberg produced *Crunch* (U.S. release title: *The Kinky Coaches and the Pom-Pom Pussycats*) and *Hot Touch* (a.k.a. *French Kiss*), directed by Roger Vadim.

Considering how much government money was being spent in the form of unpaid taxes, it's not surprising that Prime Minister Trudeau had an opinion. In his book *Midnight Matinees*, the late film critic Jay Scott describes the scene at Toronto's Four Seasons Hotel on December 15, 1980: "Prime Minister Pierre Trudeau, in black tie, a blood-red rose ever so slightly wilted on his satin jacket collar, looked pensive." He was one of the guests at "Canada's most elegant and expensive movie premiere party to date":

> As usual, the party was better than the movie to which it paid tribute, which was *Tribute* [produced by Garth Drabinsky based on a Canadian play and starring Jack Lemmon, Lee Remick, Kim Cattrall, and Colleen Dewhurst]. Taking in the furs, the diamonds, the hairdos, a journalist had commented, "Your government is in some sense responsible for all this." The prime minister smiled. "It's amazing what a few tax laws can do," he said. Then he added with a shrug, "There are now many Canadian films, but there aren't too many good ones, are there?"

In fifteen words, Trudeau had summed up the state of the Canadian film industry.

I was sad about the tax-shelter years for three reasons. First, the CFDC found itself looking to recoup its investments from the tax write-offs and not from the box office, clearly against the principles of Nat Taylor and the interdepartmental committee; second, while the write-off benefited our technical personnel and Canadian-born actors working in Hollywood, it didn't do much for Canadian stories; and third, almost all the investment funds were directed towards English features for the American market, to the point that even such important Québécois filmmakers as Claude Jutra found themselves working in the English language.

When the words *tax shelter* come up in the film business everyone thinks of *Porky's*, the only Canadian film to earn over $100 million. Funnily enough, it wasn't a tax-shelter movie and had enormous difficulty finding investors. It was "way too gross," according to Pierre David. As Stephen Greenberg described it to his father Harold Greenberg, "It's really funny but it's really raunchy." Was it really raunchier than *Sept fois par jour*? True, times had changed and the CFDC no longer invested in films that raised the public's eyebrows. Harold Greenberg had managed to convince me to invest in *Sept fois* and I suspect, had I still been at the CFDC, he would have tried to convince me to invest in *Porky's*. I would have found it hard to decline the opportunity to earn a slice of that $100 million pie. It would have improved the Corporation's bottom line immeasurably.

Once the so-called moviemakers who were in the business just for tax purposes had left the scene, producers who really wanted to entertain came to the fore. One of the most ambitious was Robert Lantos.

The doors were open and I could pretty much do whatever I wanted. One of the possibilities was to move to L.A., where a studio had offered me a development deal with an office, a secretary, and $100,000 to spend as I wished. I stayed, though, because *In Praise of Older Women* was very successful, and my thought was that if I could just duplicate this, I'd make a film on a Canadian book that appeals to me. And the actors will come and knock on my door.

Lantos's next feature, the political thriller *Agency*, was indeed based on a Canadian novel by Paul Gottlieb. It was directed by George Kaczender, who had also directed *In Praise of Older Women*, and starred Lee Majors, Robert Mitchum, Valerie Perrine, and Canadian actress Alexandra Stewart (the cast of seventy-five was probably the largest in any Canadian feature to that date). The film's budget was $4.4 million, with a $200,000 contribution from the CFDC. But, sadly, it did not perform well at the box office.

The 1979 federal election marked the end of John Roberts's tenure as minister of Communications. "I've never lost an election," he observed, "but quite often prime ministers have lost elections for me." In this case, Pierre Trudeau lost to Joe Clark, who appointed David MacDonald the next minister — the same David MacDonald who had argued so strongly for Canadian control of Canadian film investments. He had been the only MP to make a significant contribution during the debate on the original Act to establish the CFDC.

Faced with the usual confusion and lack of clarity in cultural policies, MacDonald decided to set up an advisory committee. The chairman of the Federal Cultural Policy Review Committee was to be Louis Applebaum, a respected composer from Toronto whom

John Grierson had chosen for the music scores of many wartime NFB documentaries. Applebaum and his fellow commissioners would review all the cultural sectors and hold public hearings across the country to determine new policy directions for them. I had high hopes.

In December 1979 I was watching TV at the historic moment when Réal Caouette, the leader of the Social Credit Party, stood up in the House of Commons to vote against the budget. I was hoping for a close-up of Joe Clark at this critical juncture in Canadian history, but in those days the TV coverage in the House consisted mostly of long shots from fixed camera positions. The government was defeated and had to resign. Trudeau was soon back in power and MacDonald was no longer even an MP.

John Roberts expected to regain his old job, but the Privy Council, as always, wanted to shuffle the pack, and John too became a victim of the Harvard Business School approach to business management. As Roberts recalled:

> It never crossed my mind; I just automatically assumed that I would be put back as secretary of state because I loved all of that. But they had made me minister of Environment and minister of Science and Technology, two subjects about which I knew absolutely nothing! I remember one terrible day, right at the beginning as minister of Environment, when they said to me: "Well, you'd better talk about acid rain." And I said: "What is acid rain? Because it sounds to me like some kind of rock group!" They were not amused. They thought: "Oh God. What have we been landed with?"

Francis Fox was named the new minister of Communications, and hence the minister to whom Lou Applebaum would report. As Fox noted many years later:

> Lou Applebaum remained chairman and Jacques Hébert became co-chairman. Applebaum did not want to be known as "co." He was chairman and the other fellow was "co." One of the reasons that we wanted to bring in Jacques Hébert was that we knew that if you go into cultural funding at any point in time, unless you have the support of the prime minister of the day, you're not going to get very far. So we

thought we'd like to enrich the Commission by appointing somebody who had a lot of credibility with Pierre Trudeau.

One day in early 1980, as I was working with Pierre Lamy in our Old Montreal basement office, I received an invitation to be on the jury at the 1980 Cannes film festival. The last thing I expected was to be suddenly swept away to Cannes.

The festival is always a lavish party, where show business, an endlessly fascinating subject, is the only topic of conversation. In my role as executive director, the first-class restaurants, sandy beaches, and palm trees had been but a backdrop to the hard work the festival entailed. But this year, in appreciation for the support that Canada had given it over the previous ten years, the festival organization had asked me to be a jury member. Michael McCabe — whose lack of background in film production had so worried me — had persuaded the CFDC to undertake a big advertising campaign at the 1979 and 1980 festivals in support of Canadian cinema. His media blitz worked faultlessly; *Variety* headlined its 1979 festival edition "Canada Cannes and Does." I'm sure he didn't expect that I would be the one invited to be on the jury.

I was thrilled to find myself alongside nine international jury members, including actors Kirk Douglas and Leslie Caron; Charles Champlin, film critic for the *Los Angeles Times*; Gian Luigi Rondi, director of the Venice Film Festival; and Ken Adam, art director of *Goldfinger* and other popular hits of the 1960s and 1970s. When Robert Favre Le Bret, the director of the Festival, introduced the jury to the press, he called me "l'homme a tout faire du cinéma canadien." What an elegant way to describe a cultural bureaucrat! I wasn't an internationally known director or producer, actor or film critic, but here I was in the pantheon of Cannes jurors. And I was in good Canadian company: Norman McLaren, the NFB's famous animation artist of the 1950s and 60s, had been on the jury in 1958, and in later years, so would Atom Egoyan and David Cronenberg.

All I had to do, it seemed, was go to parties and soak up the movies. Films in Official Competition were screened every day, and we had reserved seats in the balcony. At the first meeting, Kirk

Douglas, our genial chairman, recommended that we wait until we had seen at least half the films in competition before we met again. Meanwhile, I joined the Cannes audience to see the opening film, Gilles Carle's *Fantastica*, an ecological fable set to music starring Carole Laure and produced by Guy Fournier. But after I had seen some of the other features in the competition, I knew the prospects didn't look too good for a Canadian entry to win any prizes. And then it got worse: the embarrassing tax-shelter picture *Out of the Blue*, directed by Dennis Hopper (*Easy Rider*), had somehow got into the Official Competition as the entry from Canada. I can only assume that Hopper's name carried a lot of weight at Cannes.

Jurors in film festivals are expected to be discreet. Though Maqbool and I went to all the glitzy parties I never discussed the films in competition, even though I was dying to know what other people thought. The deliberations of a jury are shrouded in secrecy; only the verdicts are known.

Like all juries, we had our differences. A major one brought Kirk Douglas in from the tennis court when a jury member suggested, three days from the end of the festival, that we should call an emergency meeting and start deliberating all over again. The rest of us had made up our minds, though, and Douglas managed to quell the revolt. Finally, on the advice of Favre Le Bret, we made an *ex-aequo* decision, splitting the major prize — the Palme d'Or — between Akira Kurosawa's *Kagemusha* and Bob Fosse's *All that Jazz*. Perhaps this last-minute confusion and all the *ex-aequos* contributed to the rather lacklustre quality of the closing ceremony.

My happy surprise was the Canadian short film. When the category came up, I gave my support to Norma Bailey's *The Performer*. The film focuses on a performer preparing to go onstage. His handlers are fussing with his costume and make-up for some big show. What could it be: Opera? A circus? Mime? What? In the very last scene our performer enters Maple Leaf Stadium in Toronto, where he'll sing "O Canada" before the big hockey game. The film won the prize for best short, but *ex-aequo*, of course, with Czechoslovakia's *Krychle*. It was, as I said, an *ex-aequo* year at Cannes.

Still keeping an eye on the broad political front of Canadian cinema, I had been waiting for the CRTC to do something about licensing pay TV. The delay was later explained in the 1986 report of the task force on broadcasting policy: the CRTC "was concerned that no predominantly Canadian service could be provided that would itself contribute to achieving the goals of the Broadcasting Act, and that any such service would weaken the capacity of existing Canadian broadcasters to fulfil their obligations under the Act." In other words, the task force confirmed that it was unlikely Canadian stories would attract significant audiences to the new service.

This was not the view of the CFDC when I was there. To us, pay TV looked like a possible solution to the perennial lack of funds from Canadian theatres to finance Canadian movies. Money from Canadian box offices still went south, despite the interdepartmental committee's request that 10 percent should be left in Canada. As the CFDC saw it, a good portion of the income from pay TV could be used to finance Canadian production. And because Canadian TV was controlled by the CRTC, we thought it should establish a levy to fund the production of Canadian shows. Entrepreneurs in the broadcasting business, however, looked on Canadian-owned pay TV as simply another way of making money with U.S. programs.

Strangely enough, pay TV had made its appearance in Canada in the 1960s under the name of Telemeter, when J.J. Fitzgibbons was still CEO of Famous Players. (This was the same J.J. Fitzgibbons who in 1950 had persuaded the Department of Finance not to interfere with U.S. movie rentals in Canada by offering the Canadian Cooperation Project to a bemused C.D. Howe.) The pay TV experiment had taken place in what was then the borough of Etobicoke in Toronto. According to Larry Pilon, long-time legal counsel to Famous Players president George Destounis, Paramount had authorized Famous to invest in the installation of several thousand slot machines to be attached to TV sets so that householders could screen feature films at home. All they had to do was put the requisite amount in the slot, not unlike the gas meters of an earlier era. The experiment was not a success. Even though the sets were installed in an upper-class neighbourhood, the use of slugs instead of real coinage was widespread. The cost had reached $2 million — a not inconsiderable sum in those days — before Famous and Paramount discontinued it.

Twenty years later, in 1982, the CRTC finally licensed pay TV in Canada. At the hearings preceding this decision, many hopeful applicants submitted briefs, most of which correctly referred to the CFDC as being in favour of their idea. Pay TV was expected to give a boost to the revenues of Canadian producers. Unfortunately though, the CRTC ended up licensing eight channels based on what I could see were the applicants' overly optimistic and ill-researched revenue forecasts. It wasn't long before expectations were dashed. Two commissioners, Jean-Louis Gagnon and John Grace, had already dissented. "How many of these birds will fly?" they said. And they were right. "The launch of pay TV was a disaster," their minority report declared. "The licensees badly oversold their product." "Confused consumers were barraged by the conflicting claims of three competing services." "The early collapse of C channel shook investor confidence." Faced with more than $50 million in combined losses, the CRTC restructured the pay channels into Super Ecran, Super Channel, and First Choice.

Harold Greenberg and his brothers at Astral-Bellevue moved quickly in 1984 to acquire a controlling interest in First Choice. With pay TV under his control, Greenberg had achieved his goal of becoming "Mr. Show Biz in Canada." From a small beginning in his father's camera shop, he had become a major player in Canadian cinema as a distributor and owner of laboratories and sound recording studios. And now with pay TV his empire would continue to expand, even though his untimely death in 1996 deprived him of the chance to enjoy its full flowering.

Meanwhile, I had become the president of L'association des producteurs de films du Québec in 1981. That year the APFTQ decided that Montreal's International Film Festival — Le festival des films du monde — wasn't doing enough for Canadian and particularly Quebec cinema, and suggested that its members boycott the event.

Serge Losique, who had organized the Canadian Student Film Festival at Concordia University, had launched Montreal's second International Film Festival in 1977 as Le festival des films du monde. The festival's birth one year earlier was not without controversy in the Quebec film milieu. Losique had initially called it Le festival canadien des films du monde, but dropped the "canadien" for its second edition.

The boycott had no effect on Losique (who remains the director of the festival to this day). The Montreal public, as well as an international audience, turned out in large numbers to see the films. As president, I had to take the boycott seriously and declined all invitations for parties and premieres that year, even though it meant missing the opportunity to meet actress Gina Lollobrigida, the jury president. Luckily for Gilles Carle, his Quebec family saga *Les Plouffe* hadn't been produced by a member of the APFTQ and won a special award for Best Canadian Feature Film. Curiously, Carle also happened to be on the jury that year.

The Federal Cultural Policy Review Committee, as the Applebaum-Hébert commission was officially named, did not complete its report until 1982. Consensus was difficult to achieve among its eighteen members, who included producer Denis Héroux, writer Rudy Wiebe, artist Mary Pratt, publisher Alain Stanké, actor Jean-Louis Roux, and record man Sam Sneiderman.

The committee had held hearings in eighteen centres across the country; in total, 1,369 briefs were submitted from every conceivable cultural group, of which 512 were presented verbally. When its brief was presented in Toronto, CMPDA executive director Millard Roth and president George Heiber underlined the importance of the status quo in order to head off any talk about quotas and levies. "Exhibitors are peculiar people," observed Heiber. "They are sentimental about money. They run theatres for profit." And how do these exhibitors make profits? From the American films that the members of his association supply. It was their opinion that since the public clearly enjoy them, it would be a serious mistake on the part of any government, federal or provincial, to interrupt the flow.

As a member of the committee's staff, I had become aware of its opposition to protectionist measures. But although it made no specific recommendations about the American control of Canadian theatres or about quotas, it did recommend that "the Canadian Film Development Corporation should have its role and budget substantially enlarged so that it may take bolder initiatives in financing Canadian film and video productions on the basis of their cultural value and professional quality."

Noting that "the major foreign-controlled distributors in this country have not shown sufficient interest in Canadian films to assure a promising future to a truly indigenous production industry," the Committee also recommended that the Canadian-controlled distribution industry be given the economic strength to market Canadian films successfully to Canadian and foreign audiences through all channels of exhibition and sales. There was nothing here to compel more Canadian pictures into Canadian theatres, but at least we had made some progress since 1966, when Judy LaMarsh expressed the hope that the American-owned theatre chains would give "more than ordinary support" to the distribution of Canadian films.

James Domville, film commissioner and NFB chairman since 1979, outlined the views of that organization at a Montreal hearing. While other agency heads had surrounded themselves with senior officers and advisors, he sat alone before the committee, giving the impression that their questions would be easy to handle in a solo performance. (It reminded me of the NFB's attitude towards the Massey Commission in 1949. Ross McLean, the commissioner at the time, was all for ignoring it completely; in the tradition of John Grierson, nobody was going to tell the Film Board what to do.) Domville didn't seem to know that the creative and financial growth of the private film industry had been greatly stimulated by the general economic growth of the country, the production requirements of the private broadcasting sector, the existence of the CFDC, and tax incentives such as the CCA. The committee had heard from film people across the country yearning to express themselves on film without having to join the staff of the NFB, or wanting the chance to sell film ideas directly to government departments without getting its *imprimatur*.

Domville did not convince the committee, whose report stated categorically that:"the National Film Board should be transformed into a centre for advanced research and training in the art and science of film and video production." It added that all the film and video needs of the federal government departments, now handled by the NFB, should be filled by independent producers. The Board, firmly entrenched in the Griersonian tradition that no one told the NFB what to do, was outraged.

I wasn't even a member of the committee but I found myself accused of being somehow solely responsible for this recommendation. Jacques Godbout in particular was quite nasty to me in a colloquy organized at the NFB. He felt that the committee had ignored the NFB's contribution to Canadian cinema over the years — and once again I became aware of the significant difference between the French and English points of view. While the committee had been listening to arguments in favour of the private sector across the country, it hadn't considered that its NFB recommendation (which was rejected; the NFB is still involved in production and distribution) would have cut off what had always been a fruitful collaboration between the NFB and the Montreal film industry. On the"if you can't beat 'em, join 'em" principle, the Board's French units frequently co-produced with Montreal private producers, who were keen to get the Board's financial support. The Board's mandate to produce films in the national interest could cover a wide territory. It certainly extended to Denys Arcand's *Le déclin de l'empire américain* and *Jésus de Montréal.*

The most significant outcome of the work of the 1949 Massey Commission was the creation of the Canada Council, which to this day is the main source of financial support for Canadian writers and poets, painters and sculptors, musicians and composers, and their associated museums and art galleries. Similarly, as far as I'm concerned, the most significant outcome of the work of the Federal Cultural Policy Review Committee was recommendation number 75: "The CRTC should require private broadcasters to allocate substantial percentages of their programming time, programming budgets and gross revenues to new Canadian program production." While the Quebec private broadcasters didn't need the admonition, there was little original production by either the English private broadcasters or the private producers under contract to them.

This tied in neatly with its recommendation that the CFDC should also take bolder initiatives in the same vein. The Applebaum-Hébert report had lent its full weight to the argument, which I had first made to Gérard Pelletier years ago, that the Corporation should have the resources to finance the burgeoning Canadian television industry so that it would start telling Canadian stories.

Now it was up to Francis Fox to convince the Cabinet and the Treasury Board to make it happen.

CHAPTER 12
CHANGING CHANNELS
1980–1988

Mr. Francis Fox was responsable for getting a "big pile of money" from Ottawa for Canadian television funding and re-naming the CFDC to Telefilm Canada which reflected its new dual film and television mandate.

It's never easy to get $50 million out of any government, but we did it," laughed Francis Fox when we met to reminisce about the CFDC events of the 1980s. Perhaps it had something to do with Jacques Hébert and the prime minister.

Armed with the Applebaum-Hébert report, Fox and his deputy minister, Robert Rabinovitch, had set about increasing the CFDC's funds. The $10 million stipulated in the founding CFDC legislation had always restricted any increase in its funding, but Rabinovitch came up with a way around that: the agency could be made responsible for disbursing funds allocated to the Department of Communications for specific purposes such as investment in TV. All that was needed now was a contract between the Department and the CFDC. Fox and Rabinovitch then detailed their financial proposal for $50 million in additional program funds and began discussions with Finance Minister Marc Lalonde and his right-hand man Mickey Cohen.

"When we met with them," Fox recalled, "Lalonde was quickly onside on the question of having the pot of money established for the purpose." Lalonde agreed that the money could come, not from general revenue, but a special tax. Directed revenues are always a controversial subject in the higher levels of federal bureaucracy, and so Lalonde "made Rabinovitch and I swear that we would never say there was any connection between the cable tax and the fund," Fox recollects.

"On the night of the 1983 budget, we're listening to Lalonde make his speech. He said, 'And we're introducing a new tax on cable of 8 percent, and this money will be used to set up a much-needed broadcast production fund.' We were quite surprised that he actually said it. He was introducing a tax, which didn't make the cable people particularly happy." But it was a feather in Fox's cap and well beyond the expectations of any of the industry players. As one person put it: "I think everybody was a bit taken by surprise when we got that pile of money."

The Canadian Broadcast Development Fund opened for business on Canada Day, 1983, under the CFDC's executive director André Lamy and its chairman Ed Prévost. Committing to $50 million annually marked a giant step for both the government and the industry. Expanding the CFDC's role to administer television funds was a proposal that I had initiated in the 70s, so I got a great sense of satisfaction knowing that the government had finally recognized the importance of having Canadian stories competing with all the foreign fare in our living rooms.

The introduction of the Broadcast Fund also marked the government's recognition of the key role the private sector would play in our future entertainment industry. As Fox said at the time, "In its first five years the Fund [$250 million] should attract an additional $750 million in public and private money to the production of Canadian programming — to the considerable benefit of Canada's film and video production industry." This was the initiative that positioned Canada as a competitive global player in today's world of popular culture, with the government and the film industry working together to achieve the goal. "Central to its success will be a close partnership of effort, and indeed continuing cooperation and consultation, between the public and private sectors."

Francis Fox also continued to manoeuvre skilfully through both bureaucratic and parliamentary procedures to deliver his 1984 National Film and Video Policy. Among other things, the policy effectively decreased the responsibilities of the NFB and made the CFDC the federal government's primary film and television agency. The shift wasn't surprising, considering the NFB's failure to convince the Federal Cultural Policy Review Committee that it had any concern for the expanding Canadian film and television industries. Its main role, which it performed extremely well, was winning prizes at Canadian and international film festivals.

The essence of the National Film and Video Policy was the new direction of government assistance to the film industry. Television would become the chosen medium and a new name for the expanded CFDC had to be found. "Telefilm Canada" was a controversial choice at the time; a "telefilm" was perceived as being not quite a real film. Over the years, however, the agency has created a good reputation for itself and for the word as well. Along with its new name, $7.75 million was allotted to its annual budget to carry out a slew of new film and TV activities, including everything from script development to test marketing.

The Broadcast Fund was a harbinger of the current Canadian Television Fund's annual $200 million, which is administered by Telefilm Canada and the private sector. (This annual appropriation would stand until April 2003, when it was cut back by $50 million.) The CTF's first annual report for fiscal year 1998–99 noted that the annual $50 million from Telefilm's Broadcast Fund had been rolled into the CTF's $210 million budget. In effect, Fox's 1984 policy outlined the current parameters for public/private investment in Canadian TV. It was a landmark decision.

But even with its significant infusion of cash for Canadian television programming, the Film and Video Policy came up short of a concrete action plan for feature film distribution. Canadians still didn't have control of their own screens. The policy's rhetoric was heightened from John Roberts's day, but its target was the same: more time on Canadian movie screens for Canadian movies, whether Jack Valenti liked it or not.

"The U.S. industry," the policy read, "now has unfettered access to Canada, the largest single foreign market for its products. The Canadian industry, which has a growing and increasingly sophisticated production capability, needs greater access to its own market and both American and world markets. A more cooperative relationship can be mutually beneficial." Eerily reminiscent of Roberts's (ministers may change but departmental draftsmen go on forever), Fox's policy closed with the usual veiled threat:

On behalf of the Government of Canada, I have been authorized by Cabinet to negotiate with foreign-owned distributors operating in Canada — the member companies of the Canadian Motion Picture Distributors Association (CMPDA) — with a view to assuring:

Greater access by Canadian productions to Canadian audiences through their domestic distribution systems

Greater access by Canadian productions to the American market and other foreign markets through the worldwide distribution systems of these firms' parent companies

A greater proportion of the revenues from the Canadian theatrical market for Canadian-owned and controlled film production and distribution companies

I shall be reporting back to Cabinet in six months on the progress of these negotiations. We are hopeful that a mutually satisfactory resolution can be reached. If not, the alternative approaches adopted in other jurisdictions will represent the only way out of the present unacceptable situation.

The prospect of "alternative approaches adopted in other jurisdictions" didn't seem to worry the distribution industry. No offer was forthcoming from the CMPDA.

While the prospects for distribution were stalled, so it seemed was my own career as a producer. Projects with Pierre Lamy and later with David Patterson and Pieter Kroonenbourg just weren't moving forward. But in 1984 my outlook brightened considerably when I received an offer I couldn't refuse. It came from Richard Soames of Film Finances Ltd., a completion bond company in London, England. A bonder's role is to become familiar with all aspects of a production and to make sure that the film is completed and delivered. I could use the extensive knowledge of Canadian production I had acquired at the NFB and the CFDC; I knew all the players and would be working with both English- and French-speaking producers across the country.

I wasn't entirely a newcomer to completion bonding. In 1979 I had joined John Ross and my old friend Chalmers Adams, one of the few lawyers in Toronto specializing in show business at the time, in a Canadian completion bond company set up by Lindsley

Parsons Jr. of Los Angeles. Our first job was *Heartaches* (1981), the story of a young wife pregnant by a man other than her husband who leaves home and finds a friend in a free-spirited woman she meets on a bus. Directed by Don Shebib and produced by David Patterson, the film was shot in Georgia. And, as the bonder's representative, I was able to go on location, keeping an eye on the shoot and enjoying the camaraderie that often develops among a crew.

It was Film Finances that originated the idea of the completion bond in 1951. At that time the British film industry depended entirely on a quota system, which set the percentage of British films that had to be shown in British theatres. The National Film Finance Corporation was established to provide loans to the many small companies with limited financial resources that were producing films designed to fill this quota. But since the producers often spent all the money shooting the picture and then failed to deliver it to the distributor, the NFFC soon began to stipulate that before producers were granted a loan they had to guarantee to complete and deliver. Film Finances, with the backing of Lloyds, the insurance people, stepped in to provide this service for a fee.

Soames had provided guarantees for a few Canadian features in the late 70s, but the Canadian Audio Visual Certification Office (CAVCO) had recently ruled that foreign bonds couldn't be included in the Canadian content of the budget. (CAVCO had replaced the CFDC as the agency responsible for certifying Canadian content during the tax-shelter years.) Given that non-Canadian expenses couldn't exceed 35 percent of a film's budget, and that most of this money was allocated to expensive foreign stars, the ruling gave birth to the Canadian completion bond business. My good friend Michael Prupas, who was a senior partner in the law firm founded by Don Johnston, suggested that I join forces with Soames to create Film Finances Canada, a majority-owned Canadian corporation. It soon became a significant player in the Canadian feature film and television industry.

The myriad details of transforming a scenario into a film were endlessly fascinating to me. I soon found myself reviewing scripts

CHANGING CHANNELS (1980–1988)

177

and budgets and issuing completion bonds on a number of Canadian productions, most notably the 1985 TV movie *Anne of Green Gables*, produced and directed by Kevin Sullivan. I was pleased that Film Finances Canada was guaranteeing the completion of this quintessentially Canadian story; it was exactly the kind of film that we at the interdepartmental committee had in mind when we recommended the creation of the CFDC in the 1960s. *Anne of Green Gables* would go on to become a television series — and the most widely seen Canadian story in the world. Even today its millions of fans are glued to television sets from Japan to Middle America, Europe, and Asia. Prince Edward Island has become a mecca for international tourists who admire our virtuous Canadian heroine.

After Brian Mulroney's Conservatives swept into power in September 1984, Marcel Masse replaced Francis Fox as the new minister of Communications. Masse soon came under pressure to do something about the film industry. The bureaucratic solution was, as ever, to commission a study, and this time two representatives of the production industry, Marie-José Raymond and Stephen Roth, were called in to write a report. They called it "Canadian Cinema: A Solid Base." Like Guy Fournier in his 1982 Quebec report "Le Cinéma: Une Question de Survie et de l'Excellence (Rapport de la Commission d'Étude sur le Cinéma et l'Audio Visuel)," Raymond and Roth strongly recommended that Canada take the necessary measures to ensure that national feature films had a definite place in our American-controlled theatres.

Meanwhile, Film Finances was keeping me busy. One of the movies we bonded brought me back into contact with Rock Demers, who in 1971 had produced his first feature film, *Le martien de Noël*, with the help of the CFDC. He had remained active in the industry, mostly as a distributor. In 1983 he created Faroun Films and planned his famous series, *Tales for All*. The first film in the series, *La guerre des tuques*, was directed by André Melançon, written by Roch Carrier, and photographed by François Protat. Once again I found myself on location, this time while the final, filmic battle was fought in the Quebec countryside at Ste. Mélanie. The weapon of choice was the snowball.

Back in Montreal, another kind of battle was brewing between the NFB and Telefilm Canada over finance and jurisdiction.

The man in the middle was François Macerola, a lawyer who had joined the NFB staff in 1976 and became its boss in 1984. As such, he was the government film commissioner and, simultaneously, an *ex-officio* member of the board of Telefilm Canada. It was a conflict of interest that I hadn't foreseen in 1968 when the interdepartmental committee decided that the film commissioner should be involved in the decisions of the yet-to-be created CFDC.

Macerola's position was unique, to say the least:

> You know, at the time, we had a lot of new programs. The joke between Lamy and myself was that I was going to Ottawa to beg for one dollar for the National Film Board, and instead of giving me one dollar they would cut my budget by $100. Meanwhile, Lamy was going there on behalf of Telefilm Canada to say: "Well, stop giving me money. Don't give me more than one dollar. I don't know what to do with it." And he would receive $100. Telefilm had become the privileged instrument of the Canadian government. They were getting the money. They were in a phase of expansion, opening regional and international offices in L.A., London, New York, and Paris. They took all the international structure from the NFB.

In hindsight, Macerola smiles about the absurdity of the situation. If he hadn't done anything else, Lou Applebaum had decisively tilted the playing field.

Adding to the absurdity were the management problems that were soon to plague Telefilm. In June 1985 I read in the papers that André Lamy had resigned. He had been doing an outstanding job, but he must have been perceived as coming from the wrong political party. Some of us believed that senior positions in the

179

government weren't subject to change for the sole reason that the incumbent had some real or imagined connection with the party in opposition; Lamy's departure disabused me of this idea. "André Lamy was fired by the Conservatives and replaced by Peter Pearson," said Macerola. "And [chairman] Ed Prévost went through the same treatment: Jean Sirois replaced him. I was there as a Telefilm Canada board member, but we all remember that it was a very, very difficult time for Telefilm Canada. The two years of Pearson and Sirois were the crisis years."

In my view, Pearson had all the right qualities to justify his appointment as executive director, even though, like Sydney Newman, he was perhaps more of a creator than a cultural bureaucrat. He had been a writer and director for the NFB, the CBC, and the private sector since the 1960s, and had even directed 1972's *Paperback Hero*, one of my favourite Canadian films. Sirois must have been badly briefed either by the Privy Council or by the minister of Communications on his role as chairman of Telefilm. He really believed that he had been appointed to be the hands-on chief executive of the organization.

"The problem was that Sirois didn't know what his role was as a chair and he behaved like the executive director," notes Macerola. "Sirois didn't know that a board of directors shouldn't be involved in programming, and he wanted to be involved in programming. It wasn't a question of bad faith; it was a question of ignorance. That's what I think."

This was in stark contrast to the advice I had received from the U.K.'s John Terry at the CFDC's first meeting: "The only role of the members of the Corporation is to decide what films the money should go into and how much." The role of the executive director is to analyze the applications and make recommendations to the board. Indeed, for the first ten years I had always made sure that the members were familiar with the broad outlines of the films we were investing in. As chairman in my day, Gratien Gélinas often had strong views, but in the end a consensus was reached.

A serious disagreement between the executive director and the chairman is a recipe for disaster.

Not surprisingly, the constant bickering at the top resulted in resignations at the senior level of management. There was no control on expenditures; the system seemed unable to cope with the new money that the agency had to account for. "I remember attending meetings where one day we had a surplus of $15 million and the day after it was a deficit of $25 million," said Macerola.

The problem was further compounded by the new players — the suits. Macerola remembers that: "before, you were doing business with some small film producers — and suddenly you have in your office Radio Canada, TVA, Global, CTV." Senior executives from large corporations in the television world were a different breed altogether from the filmmakers and artists with whom the Corporation was regularly in contact. They weren't risk takers; the bottom line was more important to them than artistic merit.

The confusion soon brought the Corporation dangerously close to extinction. Its new size and clout had outstripped its administrative capacities. Jean Sirois had been seduced by smoke and mirrors and was simultaneously attempting an end run at the day-to-day operations of the executive director. The glitz and glamour of the movie business had gotten to him.

The situation got so bad that both the Canadian Association of Motion Picture Producers and L'association des producteurs de films du Québec (I was an honorary member of both) asked me to talk to the minister of Communications on their behalf. I was to point out that the industry was in disarray because of this squabble, which was all over the trade press. I was miffed that I could meet only with an executive assistant, who simply stated that the minister was already aware of the problem.

Things came to a head in spring 1985 when Macerola, Sirois, and Pearson all attended the Cannes festival. Ironically, this was the year that Denys Arcand's *Le déclin de l'empire américain* was a hit at the Director's Fortnight, won Le Prix de la Critique, and created a frenzy of a sort among Canadian journalists. The film, which centres on a group of academics intensely discussing their lives over dinner, profoundly touched audiences in Quebec.

As *Le déclin de l'empire américain* was making headlines at Cannes, *déclin* was the word used to describe the decadent reputation that Telefilm was quickly acquiring under its new leadership. Rumours of out-of-control administration and extravagant expense accounts had reached the press.

Macerola was in a good position to observe the scene:

> Poor Jean Sirois was being completely dépassé. He thought he was Mr. Cinema. He didn't know what to do. Imagine, you're a small-town lawyer in Quebec and suddenly you're in Cannes on the Croisette and you're inviting the press to dinner at Le Moulin des Mougins on the advice of your executive director, who wants to put you in the corner. I warned Jean: "Don't do that with the journalists . . . they'll eat you alive. And the day after, they'll bitch on the Croisette that you're spending public money. But nevertheless they'll all get their cognac. After that, they'll write their story, but not before the cognac." And Jean said: "Come on François, I don't believe you!" And for sure the day after, it was in every single newspaper.

Canadian newspapers were equally ripe with stories of scandal and eccentricity. Telefilm's image needed much more than a dash of lipstick — it needed a total makeover. Since there was no consensus between the executive director and the chairman, the other members of the Corporation insisted that an independent consulting firm, CGI, step in to prepare a strategic action plan. CGI assigned a woman of outstanding ability, Michèle Fortin, to plan the new administrative structure for the corporation.

The Sirois–Pearson battle ended when Pearson effectively resigned on October 12, 1987. Judith McCann was acting director for a few months before Michèle Fortin took over and held the reins for six months as she began re-establishing Telefilm's business reputation. Sirois left in April 1988. Macerola describes Fortin as the person who "saved Telefilm's ass. Absolutely."

Despite the political wrangling, remarkable films and TV shows came out of that tumultuous period. In addition to *The*

Decline of the American Empire and *Anne of Green Gables*, Patricia Rozema made her directorial debut in 1987 with her whimsical fantasy film starring Sheila McCarthy, *I've Heard the Mermaids Singing*, which also made a splash in Cannes.

One of the most impressive films of the period, I thought, was Yves Simoneau's suspenseful crime thriller *Pouvoir intime*. Produced by Roger Frappier, Claude Bonin, and Francine Foret, it stars an impressive array of Quebec name actors: Marie Tifo, Pierre Curzi, Jacques Godin, and Jean-Louis Millette. (I had provided the completion bond and, as usual, had visited the location. There I saw a security guard being nearly drowned by the bad guys inside an armoured truck!)

In late 1986 Flora MacDonald was appointed the new minister of Communications. She soon announced a new distribution policy based on the Raymond-Roth report that had been commissioned by Marcel Masse. The policy would license the importation of foreign films and thereby declare officially that Canada and the U.S. were not a homogeneous territory. Films being distributed in Canada were now to be the subject of a separate Canadian contract — a move that would finally give us control over our own screens. Hugh Faulkner, John Roberts, and Francis Fox had all tried to achieve this. Could Flora MacDonald fare better?

It didn't look good. Before the legislation could reach the House of Commons, it was leaked to the opposition and the press. Though it was hailed in the May 6, 1988 *Montreal Gazette* as "just the ticket for Canada. . . . Bravo, Flora MacDonald, you finally got the film policy exactly right," the Americans didn't think so. Jack Valenti and the CMPDA believed that the legislation went against the principles of the free trade agreement and would seriously jeopardize further negotiations. Brian Mulroney was rumoured to be saying that it was a "deal breaker."

It was partly a question of timing. At this point Mulroney was in the midst of his campaign to sell Canadians the concept of free trade with the U.S., and the last thing he needed was a policy that

183

restricted American access to the Canadian market. He was already encountering resistance from the cultural nationalists, a small but effective lobby. It was determined that the free trade agreement should not permit the U.S. to dominate our cultural scene. In their eyes, American magazines, books, films, and TV programs weren't just products like cars and canned soup, and shouldn't have unlimited access to the Canadian market. Negotiations became so tense that, in the end, both sides agreed to leave culture off the table. In this way Mulroney was able to tell Canadians that the issue had been addressed.

He didn't fool Francis Fox. "By saying that culture is not included, you're taking it out; you're leaving it out there in limbo. I would have set out the right to special measures to promote culture — not to defend culture, to promote culture — without being open to retaliatory measures."

Having successfully negotiated the free trade agreement, Mulroney called a general election. Sadly, Flora MacDonald lost her seat in the House of Commons and the film policy was lost with her.

As I watched Reagan and Mulroney singing "Irish Eyes Are Smiling" on the stage of La Capitale Theatre in Quebec City, I thought, "Valenti must be pleased to see them celebrating a deal that once again leaves the American majors in control of Canadian theatres." But I certainly wasn't smiling.

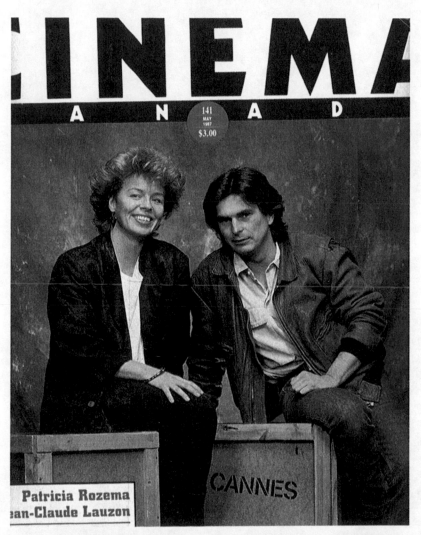

Directors Patricia Rozema (*I've Heard the Mermaids Singing*) and the late Jean-Claude Lauzon (*Night Zoo*) featured together on the cover of Cinema Canada in May 1987.

Waving from the infamous red carpet on the steps of the Palais in Cannes in 1997 are *The Sweet Hereafter* winners (Grand Prix du Jury). From left to right: Vedette Bruce Greenwood, director Atom Egoyan, star Sarah Polley, the invincible and radiant producer Camelia Frieberg and the executive director Robert Lantos.

Minister Sheila Copps surrounded by two of Canada's best internationally-known directors: (left) David Cronenberg congratulating Atom Egoyan for his win at Cannes for *The Sweet Hereafter*.

Michael and Maqbool Spencer sweep up the red carpet in Cannes.

On the beach of La Croisette for *Crash*, sits (left) one Canada's finest First Assistant Directors, David Webb (*Crash*) with tireless producer Roger Frappier who was at the festival with Cosmos. Standing are Telefilm Canada's former executives Suzan Ayscough and Bill House (1996).

Here in Hallowe'en costume as a grinning Captain Hook, Francis Fox told us in an interview that: "It's never easy to get $50 million out of any government." (See chapter 12 for his explanation).

The 6th and 7th executive directors of Telefilm Canada, Mr. Francois Macerola (left) and Mr. Richard Stursberg. The Feature Film Fund with its 5 Percent Solution was introduced in François's time and is being executed under Richard's leadership.

Quebec personalities Simon Durivage and Michel Côté share a drink and a laugh at a festival party.

Mel Hoppenheim celebrates with actor Michael Caine, an unknown lady and Jack Valenti at the Montreal World Film Festival.

Serge Losique, president of the Montreal World Film Festival celebrates with Wayne Clarkson, head of the Canadian Film Centre.

Meetings of the CFDC usually provided an opportunity for relaxation. Here Vice Chairman David Silcox and Gratien Gélinas share a joke in Vancouver with author Michael Spencer. Gratien's show business experiences often enlivened the meetings of the Corporation.

On opening night at the Toronto International Film Festival, director Piers Handling chats with Alliance Communications' vice president, Suzan Ayscough.

On Parliament Hill, Quebec star-turned-lobbyist Michel Côté explains to Canada's Minister of Finance, Paul Martin, why government funding is important to indigenous television and film production.

Also on Parliament Hill is *Due South* star Paul Gross with Minister Sheila Copps.

Prime Minister Jean Chrétien attends a screening of *The Sweet Hereafter* and is here seen with Telefilm Canada executive director François Macerola and Alliance Communications chair/CEO, Robert Lantos.

André Link (left) celebrates Telefilm Canada's 30th anniversary with its founder Michael Spencer and Board Member Jeannine Beaubien in 1998.

In the home office of Gil Taylor in 2002, author Michael Spencer looks at the old 1969 *Toronto Life* cover with Gil on the set of *Flick*.

The late Phillip Borsos will long be remembered for directing *The Grey Fox* and *Bethune: The Making of a Hero*.

Producer Gil Taylor on the cover of *Toronto Life* in a photo from the set of *Flick* in 1969. In an interview he told us he always said it would be a B-Movie and it was. Today Gil produces industrial films and videos.

Michael Spencer holds up his Genie award triumphantly! Years later, he asks: Who could ever have imagined that the original $10 million would grow to support an industry (and an art) worth more than $3 billion a year?

CHAPTER 13
THE DISTRIBUTION PAYOFF
1988–1990

On the Alliance Communications' terrace in Cannes, Alliance distribution executive Charlotte Mickie chats with *The Sweet Hereafter* director Atom Egoyan.

W hen the CFDC was established in 1968 we expected the distribution problem to solve itself. Surely,
we thought, a lot of Canadians would want to see
Canadian films. But by 1988 we knew that, whether Canadians
wanted to see them or not, films wouldn't get to Canadian screens
in significant numbers. Not only was the system geared to handle
American feature films, but thousands of Canadians were gainfully
employed in running the theatres, booking the films, shipping the
prints, creating the advertising, and carrying out the accounting and
all the other ancillary tasks in the film business (except actually
making the films). Who cared if the films were American and
North   America   was   a   single   film   market?

No doubt this was the point Jack Valenti had again forcefully
communicated to the federal government via the U.S. president.
But this time there was a difference. The CFDC had become
Telefilm. The Canadian film industry and Canadian films had
forced themselves into the national consciousness, and there were
hundreds of filmmakers out there who believed they had the right
stuff to entertain Canadian audiences. The government could no
longer simply ignore the industry.

André Link and René Malo of the Canadian Distributors
Association (a group excluding the American majors, who were all
in the CMPDA with Millard Roth) were the masterminds behind
the idea that investing in distribution would achieve better results
than investing in production. The CMPDA lobbied the
Department of Communications on the basis that well-funded distributors would not only make better decisions about the films people wanted to see, but would also be more inclined to invest in commercial productions with a chance to make money at the box office.
The idea appealed to the bureaucrats at Communications, who set
up an $85 million fund for distribution of Canadian films.

At his first press conference as Telefilm's new executive director, Pierre DesRoches, an experienced CBC-TV executive, had problems explaining how this new fund would be a better idea than Flora MacDonald's now-squelched legislation. DesRoches pointed out that the Fund would help distribution companies integrate with production companies so as to have enough movies to succeed financially. Some of these movies would of course have to be foreign. In his interview with us, Robert Lantos explained that distribution is indeed related to quantity:

> Very few films will be profitable; very few Hollywood studio films are profitable. By their own admission, the studios lose money on four out of five films. They can't recoup their costs. It's a terrible business if you look at it from that point of view. What makes it a business is the distribution side: distributing thirty, forty, or fifty films a year, acquiring a very modest portion of the production costs, charging fees off the top, and building a library to recycle the product. That's how Hollywood makes money.

And that's what the Fund was supposed to do: create a handful of studio-like Canadian companies that could make some money from distributing foreign pictures in the Canadian market and plough it back into Canadian production.

But because the government had never introduced MacDonald's proposed legislation, it wouldn't have the power to force the transfer to Canadian companies of the rights to distribute foreign (namely, American) pictures, which would have given them the volume — forty to fifty films a year — essential to make money. The only way to achieve this aim now became arm-twisting and judicious use of the distribution fund. Without a significant volume of films to distribute, however, Canadian distributors soon found that the fund was only a Band-Aid solution.

"It was a buy-out to buy peace," notes François Macerola, "because everyone was for the recommendation of identifying Canada as a national territory."

Telefilm Canada, which had the unenviable task of deciding who was going to get the money, chose fifteen distributors. In order to build a film library and earn significant revenue, these companies would purchase foreign product and invest in Canadian features. A select group — four from Montreal and two from Toronto — received the lion's share of the money, and the rest were left to vie for scraps. The big guns included four now-defunct companies: the Malofilm Group, Cinemaplus, Simcom/Norstar (Norstar is still in business), and Cinépix.

The unselected distributors immediately took action to get what they considered an equitable share. The group was mobilized by Pierre Latour, now the director of Film Tonic and a serious player with longevity and excellent taste in feature films (*Jésus de Montréal*, *The Red Violin*). In 1988 he told *Variety* that "it's not a question of being 'in' or 'out' of the select group. . . . When you look at the figures you see it's not democratic. This will effectively put the control of distribution in the hands of six big Canadian companies. All the smaller companies will be totally wiped out because they will not be able to compete."

Latour said it was a good idea to inject $85 million over five years, "but it should not apply to foreign productions. Where else in the world does a government give taxpayers' dollars to private foreign production companies for acquisition of their product?"

Their lobbying was effective, and under the intense pressure Telefilm began to spread the money around more equitably to the smaller distributors. But this destroyed the basis of the plan, which would work only if it was undemocratic and rewarded success. The idea that Telefilm and the $85 million fund were going to save the distribution business in Canada began to unravel.

As always, things were different in Quebec. Guy Fournier's report, "Le Cinéma: une question de survie et de l'excellence," was taken up by the Liberals, who in 1985 had replaced the Parti Québécois as the ruling party. Despite the failure of Mulroney's government to support Flora MacDonald's legislation (or perhaps because of it), in 1988 the Quebec government decided to take on the American majors. The MPAA hired some of the best lawyers in Quebec to argue forcefully against any limitation on the rights of their American clients to show films in Quebec theatres. The proposed legislation — much tougher than we had seen before — was passed by the National Assembly, and for the first time I was convinced that a government was going to follow a course that might just succeed: put the controls in place first and then negotiate.

The legislation passed, but Daniel Johnson, the new premier, didn't put the necessary orders in council into effect until October 1, 1988. The new regulations required all Canadian companies to subcontract their rights to a Quebec-based distributor. But the lobbying by the influential lawyers on behalf of the MPAA had had some effect: U.S. majors who distributed their own films through their own Canadian companies were exempt. In other words, the door was still wide open to the same old exploitation by the Americans. The government of Quebec had found it difficult to run counter to public demand for American features, and perhaps more so now that most of them were dubbed in French, with both versions released simultaneously.

With Canadian control of the theatrical market as far away as ever, feature film took a back seat to the TV productions financed by the Television and Broadcast Fund. Thanks to CRTC rules guaranteeing Canadian programs a place on Canadian TV, the television industry started to get a foothold in the business world.

Robert Lantos, along with partners Stephen Roth, Denis Héroux, and John Kemeny, had formed a new company, Alliance Communications, that would go on to become an international player. They were among the first to take advantage of the fund. Although Lantos had launched his career as a feature film producer, he realized that the money was in television: "The game plan was to build a studio. We weren't just going to be feature film producers who would occasionally get a project off the ground; we were going to build a distribution company, do our own foreign sales, and go into television production." Their first television series soon followed:

Night Heat was brought to us by these two guys Sonny Grosso and Larry Jacobson. They were Americans who had a deal with CBS for a low licence fee for late night. It wasn't enough to make the show, so they went to CTV; CTV sent them to us. I didn't know anything about television series, but we figured we could probably make it work if we could sell it to CTV, which we did. But the underpinning of the strategy for Alliance was that you couldn't build a real business on producing feature films. It couldn't be done. Producing feature films could be a component of a studio, but not the basis of it. We had to produce television; we had to have a distribution operation, including international sales. In due course we would have to figure out how to get into the broadcasting business and get some movie theatres. Hence, Alliance was born, and television became a big component of it.

Alliance merged television and feature film seamlessly with the quintessentially Canadian *Joshua Then and Now* (1985), written by Mordecai Richler and directed by Ted Kotcheff. It was both a four-hour CBC miniseries and a feature film that opened the 1985 Toronto Festival of Festivals and competed at Cannes. But Alliance didn't hang together very well. At the outset, Lantos thought Roth would be chairman and that all the partners would focus on building the business:

Everybody agreed with that in principle, but we all had our pet projects, and whenever anybody got his pet project off the ground, he was gone. So Kemeny got a movie and disappeared for six months. Héroux got something going and left. I could see that we weren't going to build anything this way. So in the course of the two years after Alliance was formed, one by one I had to buy my partners out. I was fiercely determined that if I was going to put the joy and the nightmare of being a producer aside in order to build a company, I was really going to do it.

So Lantos set off on his own and, until about 2000, Alliance produced many important Canadian feature films and TV series.

Telefilm now performed the same role in TV that the CFDC had pioneered in feature films: helping producers to sell their product in international television markets. It continued to negotiate co-production treaties with other countries, and added

191

television to the ones we had signed back in the 70s and 80s. Television provided a more stable source of funding than feature films and a solid base on which to build a profitable company.

But while studios and laboratories continued to expand and new ones were built, the feature film still remained the choice of filmmakers determined to make their names as artists of the cinema. And there was always the possibility that a low-budget Canadian feature would reap millions of dollars at the box office.

There were plenty of aspiring filmmakers. Atom Egoyan appeared on the scene with *Family Viewing* in 1987, followed by *Speaking Parts* in 1989 and *The Adjuster* in 1991. David Cronenberg made waves with *The Fly* (1986), *Dead Ringers* (1988), and *Naked Lunch* (1991). Both directors were well on their way toward acquiring international reputations.

In 1989 Denys Arcand returned to the international scene with his best work to date: *Jésus de Montréal*, produced by Pierre Gendron and Roger Frappier, photographed by Guy Dufaux, and starring Lothaire Bluteau. In the film, an actor who has been assigned to play Jesus in a passion play questions his supporting cast to find out if they're prepared to abandon their lives and follow him. According to Marcel Jean in *Les Cinémas du Canada*, "*Jésus de Montréal* draws a world where purity, represented here by spiritual and artistic values, is engulfed by commercial necessities and corrupted by money, fights and power games."

Once again, Arcand made Canada proud on the international circuit as critics from around the world praised *Jésus de Montréal*. Although the film lost the Palme d'Or to Steven Soderbergh's directorial debut *Sex, Lies & Videotape*, it did garner an Oscar nomination in the foreign-language category, along with many Genies, including Best Picture in 1990; substantial international sales; and the Golden Reel award as the largest grossing film in Canadian theatres that year.

The following year wasn't as sexy. Telefilm was to face the final chapter of the embarrassingly costly saga of *Bethune: The Making of a Hero*. "Neither a masterpiece nor a disaster," *Variety* declared: "it's a thorough document on the life of Canadian doctor Norman Bethune, a hero in China."

Years before, in 1976, the CFDC had invested $10,000 in Ted Allan's first-draft screenplay based on his book *The Scalpel and the Sword*. The ever-persuasive Allan had talked me out of the idea of having a producer in place before he got the money. The script would be so good, he said, that producers would be falling all over each other for the chance to make it. John Kemeny (*The Apprenticeship of Duddy Kravitz*) was first in line and persuaded Columbia to add its own sum of money to our contribution.

The CFDC was so optimistic about the film that it funded a trip to China for Kemeny, Allan, Norman Jewison (whom we hoped to convince to direct the picture), and me. The flight out — from Vancouver to Tokyo and then on to Beijing — was not an auspicious beginning, however. The Chinese airline seemed to have a lot of difficulty even finding the Beijing airport, let alone landing there. The number of aborted approaches to the runway in the rain and darkness was unnerving. The food was awful, the pilot wasn't wearing a uniform, and the cabin staff would have looked more at home in a military canteen. And after we did manage to land, the road from the airport to Beijing's only major hotel was illuminated by the occasional single bulb suspended above the pitch-dark highway.

We woke up our first morning to a city with hardly any cars but thousands of bicycles, each equipped with a tinkling bell. It was an incredible sight, and the first of many. At a time when few Westerners had been to China, our expedition was to prove utterly fascinating.

Our Chinese hosts had packed our itinerary with sightseeing attractions — the tomb of Mao Tse-tung in Tiananmen Square, the Great Wall of China, the Ming tombs. We also visited the hospital in Shichuajang where Bethune had worked and his grave in the military cemetery there. Our mode of transportation was a convoy of three cars, one of which carried the staff to service our needs in the government rest houses where we stayed.

In the villages we were usually invited to have a meal. We would be seated outside on hard wooden benches around a long table, along with the village elders, our interpreters, and our conducting officers. Following the meal came the inevitable speeches about the accomplishments of the People's Republic in that region; in one instance we heard far too many statistics about the glorious dam that had been constructed nearby. Our hosts would also pay tribute to Bethune, with much praise heaped on Allen for bringing the story of a Chinese hero to the West. (Bethune is pronounced something like "Betchuan" in Chinese. I would soon recognize the word in the speeches, the translations of which seemed even longer than the originals.)

One of our trips was to Yenan, which became the Communist armies' headquarters after their epic 6,000 Mile Long March in 1934 and 1935. We visited a cave where Mao used to work when he was there; its open side was covered by a wooden wall, neatly carpentered to fit the natural opening of the cave, with windows made of what looked like rice paper. Mao's desk and books were kept in perfect condition.

I began to find visiting all these historic sites a bit of a bore and fell into the role of the errant schoolboy, dragging behind the group and ducking off to look for birds. I did see a Great Spotted Woodpecker, but in doing so, embarrassed my colleagues when our hosts had to send someone to find me.

Throughout the trip I could see Jewison assessing the logistics of making a Hollywood epic in China. On our way home we were treated to a superb dinner in Hong Kong by a local film distributor, who was overwhelmed by the presence of this famous director whose films had been big successes in theatres there. Ted Allan didn't seem to mind not being the centre of attention for once.

Upon my return to Canada, I found that *The Globe and Mail* had got hold of the story of our expedition. Depressingly, the article was headlined "Chinese Are Cool on Bethune Film." At the same time I heard from Kemeny that, owing to scheduling conflicts, Jewison had decided not to direct the film. I wonder, though, if he foresaw the fate that awaited the filmmaker who took on the making of this epic.

Years later I picked up Martin Knelman's 1987 book *Home Movies*, in which he recounts the making of *Bethune: The Making of a Hero*:

> Almost from the beginning of the Canadian government's involvement in the feature-film business, from the creation of the Canadian Film Development Corporation in 1968 through its later metamorphosis into the TV-oriented Telefilm Canada, successive executive directors, with their scrambled mandate to be half Ottawa bureaucrat, half imitation-Hollywood tycoon, had made seemingly fruitless expeditions to Beijing and L.A. trying to get the dream project off the ground.

Knelman puts his finger on the problem that had plagued and will continue to plague all government enterprises designed to invest in projects that are both cultural and commercial. But the Chinese government did finally commit to the dream project. Now it was going to be made, no matter what.

John Kemeny withdrew and was replaced by Nicholas Clermont and Pieter Kroonenburg. Donald Sutherland, who had played the role of Bethune in a well-received CBC TV show, had come aboard early on and at one point seemed to be the driving force behind the film. Eventually the money was found, mostly from Telefilm, and a French co-producer signed on. Shooting finally started under Philip Borsos, who had directed 1978's *Grey Fox*, one of the memorable films produced with CFDC assistance.

Knelman summarizes the monumental problems that plagued Clermont after Borsos had begun shooting:

> Doing a co-production with the Chinese was a tremendous ordeal. Hours had to be spent translating conversations. Equipment that was supposed to be available wasn't, and had to be flown in at the last minute. Catering arrangements fell through; there were no phones and

no drinkable water on the set, and people started to get sick. Shooting fell behind schedule; there were huge disagreements about what script changes should be made. Although Hemdale, the company that distributed *Platoon*, bought U.S. rights for $2.5 million, there were still serious questions about what might happen if *Bethune: The Making of a Hero* ran out of money before the film was finished. Everyone involved would have different accounts of what went wrong and who was to blame, but the one thing they could all agree on was that filming *Bethune: The Making of a Hero* had turned into the ultimate Canadian movie nightmare.

The film's final budget was $15 million, with a contribution of $3 to $4 million from Telefilm. The fiasco continued right up until the premiere at the Montreal film festival in August 1990. The reviews were mixed, though everyone agreed that Donald Sutherland's performance was stunning. And, despite all the money and dedication of the cast and crew under almost impossible conditions, the film's only award was the 1991 Genie for Best Costume Design.

I was glad *Bethune: The Making of a Hero* finally made it to the screen. I'm not convinced, though, that it did him justice. Some heroes are enhanced by brilliant movies; I'm sure there's still one out there waiting to be made about Bethune.

THE DISTRIBUTION PAYOFF (1988-1990)

CHAPTER 14
AGAINST ALL ODDS
1995 ONWARDS

Cinémaginaire producer Denise Robert on the red carpet in Cannes, May 200[...] just after *Les invasions barbares* won for Best Director (Denys Arcand) and B[...] Actress (Marie-José Croze).

My responsibilities in the completion bond business continued to provide a marvellous means of keeping in touch with the film industry in Canada, as I travelled across the country and sometimes abroad to look in on the movies that Film Finances Canada was bonding. Many of them have disappeared from distributors' catalogues, but I still treasure the memories of these location assignments.

In *Finding Mary March* (1988), Andrée Pelletier (who had starred in Gille Carle's *Les mâles* in 1970) plays a photographer in search of the tomb of a Beothuk princess whose entire tribe had long been exterminated by white Newfoundlanders. Shooting in remote Buchans, Newfoundland, was challenging, and director Ken Pittman didn't help matters by expecting two untamed ravens (provided by local Aboriginals) to perform on cue.

The Tadpole and the Whale, about a young girl living on the St. Lawrence whose closest friends are a whale and a dolphin, was shot on Quebec's north shore in 1987. One of Rock Demers's *Tales for All* helped launch the career of Marina Orsini, who subsequently became one of the best-known performers on the Quebec scene (and star of *Les filles de Caleb*).

In 1990 I found myself in a spectacular treeless mountain valley in Grimentz, Switzerland, where Lea Pool was directing *La demoiselle sauvage*, in which a young woman running away from her past hides in the mountains until she's found by a man who helps her start life anew. The film was produced by Denise Robert and Daniel Louis, with Georges Dufaux as director of photography. (I think I almost made a birdwatcher out of Louis; he spotted a pair of Alpine Choughs flying past a crag way above us and we stopped to have a look.)

The family drama *The Lotus Eaters* (1993), produced by Sharon MacGowan, directed by Paul Shapiro, and starring

199

R.H. Thompson, was filmed on Galiano Island, B.C. From a birder's point of view, I was pleased to see a Red-necked Grebe in the Trincomali Channel. From the bonder's point of view, the location proved anxiety-producing when, in the middle of the shoot, the ferry went on strike. Since the rushes still had to be delivered to a laboratory in Vancouver every day, the producers chartered a floatplane — an extra expense, which always makes the bonder nervous.

The location shoot of *Les fous de bassan* (1987) took me to another island, L'Ile Bonaventure, a ferry ride from Gaspé. Based on a novel by Anne Hébert, the film was directed by Yves Simoneau (*Napoleon, Nuremburg*, etc.) and produced by Claude Héroux. Again a problem with the ferries! This time the ferry operators were quite happy to keep working — as long as they were paid twice the usual rate to convey the crew from the mainland to their work each day. The producer, needless to say, had a gun to his head. I've noticed over the years that fees, wages, rentals, leases, and the price of anything else rises automatically if it becomes known that there's a film company involved. Making a movie on a shoestring is the lot of the average Canadian producer, but the public wrongly assumes that there's always plenty of money around when films are being shot.

In October, 1989, there were Jackdaws flying around the tenth century Benedictine Abbey of Mont Majour which stands on a bluff overlooking the flatlands of the Rhone Delta. Here, in Van Gogh country, I was keeping a eye on *Vincent & Me* with Rock Demers. Another in the *Tales for All* series, it was Mike Rubbo's fantasy about a young Quebecoise who dreams of learning how to paint under the tutelage of the man himself in the vineyards and orchards of the camargue.

André Forcier's 1988 *Kalamazoo* is a *film d'auteur* — a particularly strong genre in Quebec — of a fantastical voyage made in a small boat from Montreal down the St. Lawrence to the French islands of St. Pierre and Miquelon off the southern coast of Newfoundland.

The script called for the actors to wade ashore when they arrived, but the water in Newfoundland is far too cold in December. Funny, though, how easily Bahia Honda Island in the Florida Keys can look like Newfoundland when the camera faces the horizon. While Forcier and his producer Jean Dansereau filmed the scene there I kept a bonder's eye on the shoot and a birdwatcher's eye on a pair of Ruddy Turnstones on the beach.

Far away from the Florida Keys, François Macerola was dealing with the routine problems of Telefilm Canada — the major one being a lack of funds. Despite the "pile of money" that Francis Fox had obtained for the Canadian Broadcast Development Fund in 1983, the industry had expanded to the point that the $50 million annual allotment was insufficient.

A significant change for the better occurred in 1996 when Sheila Copps succeeded Michel Dupuy as minister of Canadian Heritage. Unlike Dupuy, who had insisted on keeping Telefilm's appropriation at the same level, Copps immediately saw the political advantage in supporting the television industry, and set to work with Macerola to find new money for private sector production. As Macerola explained later:

> At the time the government wasn't ready to inject new money into existing departments and agencies, but it *was* interested in joint private/public organizations. I'm quite sure that's how Madame Copps succeeded. She convinced the government to fund a new organization, financed from both public and private sources, to provide funding for television. That way she did indirectly what she could not do directly. The result was $100 million annually over a five-year period in the Canadian Television Fund.

With Macerola on board and Sheila Copps as the minister, Telefilm's thirtieth anniversary in 1998 was celebrated in style (my co-author Suzan was the architect of all the events). The high point for me was a dinner at the Westin Mont-Royal hotel in February. Over 400 tickets were sold, and it was impossible to get a seat the night of the big event if your place wasn't reserved. Many of the

AGAINST ALL ODDS (1995 ONWARDS)

players in the film business joined Telefilm's senior staff and its executive directors, including the four who had briefly been acting executive directors. I was happy to meet them all again, especially André Lamy, who had taken over during the difficult time following the resignation of Michael McCabe in 1980 and had provided the administrative base for the Corporation's new course as an investor in the television industry. Judith McCann had been an acting director, also at a difficult time of transition in 1987. (But what I particularly remember is her role as an officer in the Information Division of External Affairs in 1973 when I had made the serious error of inviting India's minister of Information and Broadcasting to visit Canada. The responsibility of reprimanding me for this breach of protocol — only ministers invite ministers — had fallen on her. I was suitably chastened, yet gladly remained her friend. She later became the head of the South Australia Film Corporation, which I had had a hand in creating on my trip to Australia in 1973.) There were many in the Salle des Saisons that evening who had seen the opportunities in the Canadian film industry and had prospered in it. I wondered how I'd had the good luck to be there when it all began.

In that same year Telefilm received another honour — a special Genie awarded by the Academy of Canadian Cinema and TV for its outstanding contribution to Canadian cinema. Chairman Robert Dinan, Macerola, and I accepted the award at the annual ceremony in Toronto, which was broadcast the following day on the Bravo! network.

Macerola was now well into his term as executive director, and Sheila Copps was so pleased with his work that she appointed him to represent the film industry on a Canadian trade mission to China. But just as he was approaching the Great Wall he got a call from home. The Corporation was hitting a wall of its own. The new Canadian Television Fund (which Telefilm co-administered) was over-committed by $20 million. Astonishingly, some of Canada's most popular and successful TV series (including *Traders* and *Due*

South) were about to be locked out of government money. Producers of these shows were in a state of shock. Macerola wisely boarded a flight right back to Canada.

It was worse than he thought. Students hired by panicked producers were putting up tents on Montreal's downtown McGill College Avenue and planned to camp from the spring until the fall to be first in line for the next round of handouts from the CTF's first-come, first-served Licence Fee Program. Summer-long lineups were not exactly what the minister had in mind when she had announced increased television funding for quality Canadian programming two years earlier. According to an insider at the department of Canadian Heritage, when the tent story hit the papers Copps emerged from her office and snapped: "Get those people off the streets!"

The public and private sectors of the new Canadian Television Fund had different objectives. The $100 million private Licence Fee Program was already in place, and at least functional, when Copps arrived. The argument was about how the additional $100 million of the Equity Investment Program (administered by Telefilm) should merge with the first-come, first-served fund. The two drastically different programs just didn't mix. The Licence Fee Program was the one with the deadlines. Telefilm's Equity Investment Program didn't care about deadlines so much as quality. Moreover, the two sides were unable to agree on which funds would be used to finance which shows. Macerola sat down with the TV executives on both sides to work out an equitable and transparent system that would supposedly guarantee this wouldn't happen again! At the end of the day, both CTF Programs adopted mutually agreed upon deadlines and quality standards.

By this time Quebec feature films were once again flourishing. When the government had originally licensed private television in Canada in the 1960s, the English side had been reluctant to undertake the production of entertainment shows for an audience accustomed to American programming. This hadn't been the pattern on the French side, where the newly licensed private channel immediately launched more French-language programs to compete with Radio-Canada. This need for French-language stories was duplicated in feature films.

Feature film production in Quebec had dropped in the early 80s after the tax-shelter money had mostly gone to English-language productions. But Quebec features never completely disappeared, and Francis Mankiewicz's *Les bons débarras* (1980), photographed by Michel Brault, had achieved a mythic status among Quebec features. (Sadly, Mankiewicz did not live to enjoy the reputation he had begun to acquire with this film. He died of cancer in 1993, but left an important film legacy in his wake.) Produced by Claude Godbout and Marcia Couelle, the film starred Charlotte Laurier as a little girl jealous of the attention her mother pays to her simpleton, alcoholic uncle.

By the mid-80s the Quebec film industry had bounced back, with Denys Arcand's *Le déclin de l'empire americain* (1986) and Jean-Claude Lauzon's *Un zoo la nuit* (1987) leading the way. Prolific director Jean-Pierre Lefevbre had twenty feature films under his belt by the end of the 80s, and Roger Frappier (*Le déclin*, *Un zoo*, *Jésus de Montréal*) was the most important Quebec producer of the time.

Jean-Claude Lauzon turned out to be Quebec's *enfant terrible*. His second film, *Léolo*, was invited to the Official Competition in Cannes in 1992, where he was reportedly so vulgar to a jury member that he eliminated his own brilliant film from serious consideration for any award. I had been a nervous completion bonder on *Léolo*, knowing Lauzon's reputation for single-mindedly pursuing his artistic ideals with no thought for soaring costs. Aimée Danis and Lise Lafontaine were the ideal producers for his impetuous talent, however, and the film was completed on time and on budget, if only by a hair. I visited one location where Lauzon was shooting a scene illuminated by hundreds of candles, an interesting challenge for the director of photography, Guy Dufaux (brother of Georges).

My presence was required in order to make sure Lauzon knew that exceeding the budget would have dire consequences. He seemed to take me seriously, and I found him to be polite and rather quiet. I was saddened to learn of his death when a small plane he was piloting crashed in a forest in northern Quebec in August 1997.

Other directors in Quebec with whom I had a passing relationship on set as a completion bonder included Pierre Falardeau (*Le party*) and Claude Jutra, whose 1985 *La dame en couleurs*, produced by Pierre Lamy, was his last feature before his own tragic death resulting from Alzheimer's disease. I also had the privilege of meeting Jean Beaudin (*Being at Home with Claude*) and Michel Brault, whose 1994 *Mon ami Max* gave me an opportunity to meet Geneviève Bujold again, twenty years after the CFDC had financed *The Act of the Heart*.

Telefilm's thirtieth anniversary party had given Sheila Copps the perfect platform to announce a new feature film initiative and appeal to the industry to submit ideas. Four months later her staff issued a position paper (cultural bureaucratese for a plan), in which she asked a blue-ribbon group of film experts to study as a basis for a new beginning.

I was filled with nostalgia as I read the paper that summarized 110 submissions from across the country. I had seen it all before, but like a fire-horse champing at the bit upon hearing the alarm, I swiftly accepted Copps's offer to sit on the Feature Film Advisory Committee (FFAC). I would be joining forces with a new generation in the film industry, ready to try once again as Nat Taylor had in the 60s to make Canadian features a part of the Canadian entertainment experience. The committee included several old friends, in particular André Link, who had now sold his company to Lion's Gate but was still actively working in the industry; S. Wayne Clarkson, with whom I organized the visit of an Indian delegation to Canada in 1978 and who was now the executive director of the Canadian Film Centre; and Denise Robert, Robert Lantos, and Michael Donovan, all of whose features I had bonded.

205

The FFAC's final report (entitled "The Road to Success") was stylish and well laid out, with still photos from such recently released features as *The Red Violin* and *The Sweet Hereafter*. Quotes from Sheila Copps, Atom Egoyan, Claude Jutra, and Gil Cardinal represented Canada; George Bernard Shaw, William Randolph Hearst, and Sam Goldwyn the rest of the world. (I wonder how long it took them to find Shaw's zinger, "The moral is, of course, that the state should endow the cinema as it should endow all forms of art.")

The report's recommendations were issued in a press release. The first recommendation — that "the federal government should amend the production services tax credit to ensure that only Canadian feature film producers ... are permitted access to the program" — created no problem at all in Quebec. But it was a different story on the West Coast, where B.C. technicians and performers protested vigorously. Their jobs depended on American productions, and if the tax credits were cut, the productions would be too. Their protests were soon taken up in the East, and the idea was eventually dropped. It was becoming clear to me that, if it came to a choice between jobs and homegrown Canadian films, jobs would win every time.

The other recommendations were well received by the entire industry, of course. They included $50 million for a new feature film fund and consolidation of another $53 million from other federal sources to bring the total to a nice-sounding $100 million for Canadian feature films. I'd like to think that I had some influence on the suggestion that up to 80 percent "should flow through an automatic trigger based on box office receipts and international success." Basing government grants on box office success had been the essence of the Eady plan in the U.K., back when the CFDC was still in the planning stage in the 60s.

On the always-thorny question of distribution, the report recommended that "the Canadian distribution sector and marketing of Canadian films should be strengthened through regulatory or legislative options." Further clarification was provided in two foot-notes:

> 13. Michael Donovan represented the position that either quotas or tax-based incentives in the distribution and or exhibition sectors could be given further consideration.
>
> 14. Michael Herman of the Motion Picture Theatre Associations of Canada did support further review of the issues relating to the distribution of non-proprietary films in Canada but did not feel that the legal, financial, business, and political considerations had been sufficiently analyzed during the process to permit him to support any specific recommendations by the Committee.

In a nutshell, the committee did not recommend a clear legal sanction on the importation of foreign motion pictures into Canada. Only this would have persuaded Jack Valenti to pay attention. Once again, additional funds had been the solution instead of restrictions on American films.

True to form, Robert Lantos was first in line to take advantage of this newly available money. He had long ago decided to stay in Canada, and now he went one step further. He would produce a film about, starring, and made by Canadians, and above all, one that Canadians would find entertaining. He knew of Harold Greenberg's vision for *The Apprenticeship of Duddy Kravitz*, but his plans didn't include American distribution.

Lantos had produced the hit comedy TV series *Due South*, star-ring Paul Gross as a Mountie. Canadian audiences loved the show, as did those in the U.S. and in sixty-two other countries, including the U.K., Australia, and Germany. Now the multi-talented Gross wanted to write and direct a feature called *Men with Brooms*, a comedy about the Canadian sport of curling. Molly Parker, Leslie Nielsen, and, of course, Paul Gross starred. Released in Canada with a well-executed publicity campaign in spring 2002, its box office reached $4 million by the end of the summer, an excellent figure for English Canada (but nothing like the Quebec box office smashes *Séraphin, Un homme et son péché* or *Les boys I, II,* and *III*).

When I visited his lavish office, Lantos was high on the recent success of *Men with Brooms*, especially because it wasn't only the Canadian story but also the Canadian publicity campaign that was getting people into the theatres.

Lantos had this to say:

> The naysayers, many of whom own the media in this country, will say: "Canadians aren't interested in seeing Canadian movies." They say: "The population isn't interested, so let's not waste our time and money trying to do the impossible." Well, they're fucking wrong. No movie is more Canadian than *Men with Brooms*. There is an audience out there. You know what the biggest opening weekend gross was on *Men with Brooms*, the number one theatre? It was in Kanata, outside Ottawa, and the number two theatre was in Sudbury. Number three was the Chinook in Calgary. Many of the people going to see it have never seen a Canadian movie.
>
> When we launched Showcase [a Canadian specialty channel] we discovered that 85 percent of those questioned from Halifax to Vancouver had never once seen a Canadian movie in a movie theatre. 85 percent! Not once in their lives! My point is that almost all English Canadian films are made for a narrow, elite audience. I don't think you can expect a mainstream audience to come to an edgy, independent film, which has a deep dark sinister ending. People want to have fun. They want entertainment: they don't want to suffer when they see a movie. They want to enjoy themselves.

By the 1990s there was another contender for the role of Canadian movie mogul: Michael MacMillan, Lantos's former competitor and the chairman and CEO of Atlantis. His office is on the fifteenth floor of a Bloor Street building (as it happens, Nat Taylor's office had been in the same building in the 1960s when Twentieth Century Theatres had their offices there). He launched Atlantis Films in 1978, the year I left the CFDC. It had been a year before that when MacMillan and his original partners, who'd been friends at Queen's University, decided to form a film company called Atlantis Films. He recalls:

> We weren't burdened with any relevant knowledge or acquaintances or experience or money. In 1980 we made a half-hour drama called *The*

Olden Days Coat based on Margaret Laurence's book. We hired a nine-year-old girl called Megan Follows to play the lead [she went on to star in *Anne of Green Gables*]. We raised $138,000 to make it.

By 1982 we thought that adapting Canadian short stories, books, and poems was a great thing, so we set about making six half-hour adaptations of Canadian short stories. The Royal Bank, which had loaned us I think $30,000 towards making these six films, called in the loan. We had no flexibility; our credit cards were all up to the top. We were totally screwed.

We heard, though, of a thing called the Canadian Film Development Corporation. We didn't know what it was, and we'd been making films for four and a half years by this point. I'd never met anyone at the CFDC, so we went to the Toronto office and explained who we were and what we were doing. "We're toast, basically," I said, "and here's what we need." The fellow went off into another room, and came back fifteen minutes later and said: "Fine. You're on. Fifty thousand bucks." That afternoon we were able to call up the shoot and tell them to "Keep going! We can pay the crew!"

MacMillan noted that it was Bill House in the CFDC's Toronto office who had been able to offer the lifeline. The film was *Boys and Girls*, the only Canadian short to win an Academy Award for drama. I find it hard to believe that MacMillan didn't know about the CFDC, but I was glad to hear the story because the CFDC had swiftly and effectively saved the day, something I had prided myself on since the beginning of the Corporation.

Atlantis also realized that it would have to focus on television production and distribution to keep afloat, and then concentrate on movies further down the line once the company was prospering. My personal favourite among the projects of this period was *A Child's Christmas in Wales*, from the poem by Dylan Thomas. I am a great admirer of Dylan Thomas, more so perhaps because I once spent an evening with him in London in 1941. It wasn't a chance encounter; a friend of mine, a documentary producer, introduced us. We spent a long evening drinking Guinness in a pub on Wardour Street called The Dog and Duck, discussing the state of the world and the sad lot of writers doing narrations for British documentaries on the war effort.

209

By the mid-90s, Atlantis Films and Alliance Communications Corporation were the two major production companies supplying the English-Canadian broadcasters with programming. A merger seemed inevitable. MacMillan remembers:

> It was in 1996. Robert Lantos started by saying: "Why doesn't Alliance buy Atlantis?" And I said to him: "You've got the right concept but the names are backwards. We'll buy you." It was a conversation that would start and not finish. One of us would say something and four months later the other would reply. This went on until finally, by late '97, it was clear that it was going to happen. From January '98 until July '98 it was full steam, focused on doing it.
>
> The reason I wanted to buy Alliance and merge the two companies was that, number one, the most important thing was to get a broadcast platform that was big enough; and number two, I wanted to get us into the movie producing and distributing business. There was one effective way to do that: buy the company.

The unexpected merger of the two archrivals in July 1998 took the industry and stock market watchers by complete surprise. During the months of top-secret negotiations, Lantos and MacMillan had used the code names Pluto and Venus so that no one, including the lawyers' assistants, knew who the mystery clients were. The merger made Venus the new boss of "the 12th-largest film and TV studio in North America, with combined revenues of $927-million and assets of $850-million for the current year," according to *The Globe and Mail.* "The two men were a study in contrasts at the announcement of the merger," the article went on. "The lean, preppy Mr. MacMillan sat bolt upright, handling each question briskly and eagerly." As for "the feline Mr. Lantos," said the *Globe,* "the Pluto tag places him as far from the centre as possible without dropping him out of orbit. He will no longer have an office or even be a director of the company. But in addition to a settlement that could leave him $50-million richer, he will produce films financed by Alliance Atlantis for at least three years."

On the feature film side of Alliance Atlantis, the new corporation was fortunate that Lantos's ever-feisty and outspoken long-time partner Victor Loewy went along with the merger deal. Loewy became the CEO of the newly named Motion Picture Distribution Group of Alliance Atlantis.

Loewy supported the merger because he knew his best friend was "doing what he wanted, which is to get out of this business and back into producing." Loewy and Lantos had been partners in one way or another since their student days at McGill. (One of their first assistants remembers when Lantos, still in tip-top shape from his water polo years, asked Loewy, then a short, skinny student, if he could borrow some change for a cup of coffee. When Loewy told him to "get his own money," Lantos playfully wrestled him to the floor, grabbed him by the ankles and turned him upside down, shaking him until enough coins fell out of his pockets.) Their first distribution venture in those crazy, idealistic days when neither of them had much money was bringing a series of short films to Canada called *The Best of the New York Erotic Film Festival*.

When Alliance was in full expansion mode Loewy eventually followed Lantos to Toronto, turning over the mainly French-speaking distribution operations to Guy Gagnon's dynamic leadership. Alliance was a significant force not only in the Quebec market; it had strong connections in the rest of Canada and internationally as well. MacMillan clearly had his eye on this component of Alliance. It would be part of Alliance Atlantis, a Canadian "major" just like a studio in Los Angeles.

When I met MacMillan in 1984 I had considered him as simply a bright young filmmaker, yet he obviously had the business instincts to become the kind of English-language entrepreneur I'd hoped the original CFDC would foster. At one point in the 70s I had even organized a meeting in Montreal with all the Canadian distributors — including André Link, John Basset Jr., and Martin Bochner — suggesting that they consider merging. But I knew my idea was doomed when each person subtly indicated that he wouldn't accept a subordinate position under any of the others. Another quixotic idea from the CFDC — not the leader but the banker of the Canadian film industry. It would take twenty-five years for market forces to create two production and distribution companies that would eventually merge and at least make the American majors pay some attention.

Alliance Atlantis isn't only a production and distribution company; it has also acquired a number of theatres. In this respect, MacMillan is rather the mirror opposite of Nat Taylor, who began his career owning theatres and wanted to be a producer so that he could make films to show in them.

MacMillan has a measured view of the Canadian film industry's future:

> I think the prospects both for motion pictures and TV, in terms of true Canadian stuff, are okay. Tepidly okay. I'm not jumping up and down screaming. I think we're in a reasonable position, we being Alliance Atlantis, because we have resources of international distribution and we have, quite frankly, quite a bit of power in terms of screens. We're probably the biggest booker of screens in the country. We have more market share than any American major in Canada — 19 percent currently.

What does this mean for aspiring Canadian producers whose ideas have survived Telefilm's evaluation process and been made into movies ready for Canadian theatres? Will Canadian-owned theatres automatically guarantee screens for their movies? MacMillan is pragmatic, as always:

> Screen access is not an issue, nor is it a solution. I know that everybody likes to blame it on [lack of screen access], but it really isn't the problem. I don't believe that any Canadian film of marketable ability or quality has been unable to get the screens that it needed. Maybe it didn't have any marketing money and didn't have an ad campaign. It didn't tell anybody it was coming. Maybe it wasn't a true theatrical motion picture, but was something else, like a TV movie masquerading as a theatrical motion picture and, God knows, we've had lots of those over the years. Maybe it wasn't really something you were going to pay ten or twelve bucks to see in a cinema.

From original entrepreneur Nat Taylor to major-studio honcho Michael MacMillan the message remains the same: a film industry is, first and foremost, a commercial enterprise. People have to think they're going to be entertained, or they just won't come.

This famous aphorism must have been much in the mind of Richard Stursberg, the seventh executive director of Telefilm Canada, when he took over in January 2002. Very much at home in both broadcasting and the Ottawa bureaucracy, and fluent in French, Stursberg had been assistant deputy minister in the Department of Communications long before he was appointed chair of the CTF. Making the Feature Film Fund work effectively on the English side was the major challenge he had to face in his new assignment. Stursberg soon made his expectations publicly known by proposing the 5 percent solution: "To establish the goal established by Canada's new feature film policy of 5 percent of box office going to Canadian features we must all focus relentlessly on success," Stursberg said in a speech called: "Audience Building in Canada - Can we do it?" He added that the Corporation would: "need to support a range of genres with more comedies, more family movies and kids' pictures, more thrillers and romances," and concluded that Telefilm's "priority for Canadian feature films is simple - it is all about building audience."

The goal to achieve both cultural and commercial success hasn't changed. In an interview, Stursberg reflected upon the canyon between the French and English markets. On the French side, Quebec films now garner 16.5 percent of the market share while English features have difficulty reaching 2 percent. Stursberg's solution was to change the rules: "We developed an asymmetrical policy that was not based on politics but on market realities," he said, adding that Telefilm now requires that Canadian distributors make a written P&A commitment (prints and ads) before it will invest. "We want to see numbers before we invest," Richard said. "The producer has to show us that the distributor really believes in the film and we measure that by how much money he will invest himself." I first became aware of this principle in the 1960s when John Terry, the head of the NFFC was advising the CFDC on its investment policies.

213

Mambo Italiano, directed by Émile Gaudreault, produced by Denise Robert and Daniel Louis, and distributed by Equinoxe Films, is the first film in theatres that met those tough new distribution rules. Its box office has already exceeded $2 million in Quebec. But the crucial test will come in the fall of 2003 when the English version will be released simultaneously in the U.S. and Canada after a premiere at the Toronto International Film Festival. "English producers are trying to bring us more commercial films now that the rules have changed," Richard said.

In a recent Canadian Business magazine Denis Seguin observed that: "If the Canadian film industry can agree on one thing, it's that Telefilm's balancing act has yet to be perfected. Stursberg is counting on the 5 percent solution to deliver that balance." More specifically, the executive director said the "real targets" for 2005 are 4 percent of the English market, and 12.5 percent of the French (which is only one-seventh of the whole market). I wish them both well, the producers and the distributors. But it is not going to be easy. Cultural bureaucrats have as much trouble as anyone else determining what the public wants. Deepa Mehta (*Sam and Me, Hollywood Bollywood, The Republic of Love*) has it right: "I think it's very difficult to make a film and say: 'okay, I am going to make a commercial film'. My father was a film distributor in India and he always said: 'There are two things you never know about. One is when you are going to die, the other how well a film is going to do."

The Canadian film industry continues to expand and with it the industrial infrastructure of studios and editing suites, backed by an ever-growing cadre of skilled technicians. A recent edition of the *Director's Guild* magazine quotes Robert Lantos and several others about where we should go from here. One way we're certainly not going to go, they say, is establishing a blockbuster feature film industry with Canadian funds and Canadian resources.

But if we don't have many Canadian stories to enjoy in our theatres, we at least know that Canadians are making a significant contribution to the international theatrical industry as directors, actors, directors of photography, set designers, and owners of large studio complexes. In 1971 we were impressed when Eric Till directed *A Fan's Notes* in Toronto with a Canadian crew and the support of a major American studio. Nowadays, shooting a picture in Toronto draws protests from Los Angeles-based film unions. Indeed, the Director's Guild of America and the Screen Actors' Guild launched a campaign to take back Canada's service production, or "runaways," in the winter of 1998–99. According to Donald Sutherland, American crews sport sweatshirts featuring a maple leaf in a red circle with a red diagonal line through it. It's considered bad form to wear them when he's on set, but they still do.

There will always be entrepreneurs, directors, writers, and performers who want to tell Canadian stories. I like to think they had their greatest success in Canadian theatres in the 1970s. Even today we manage to come up with two or three films a year that let us continue to believe that, hanging on by our fingernails, we have a feature film industry in English Canada. The lessons of history are learned every day, and one of them is that an independent film's chances of becoming an international success are minuscule or nonexistent. Fortunately this fact won't discourage those Canadian filmmakers who continue to believe that if we haven't succeeded in creating a feature film industry in Canada by now, it's only a matter of time.

But there is no doubt that we *have* succeeded in Quebec. *Les boys* and *Séraphin, Un homme et son péché* (which brought home $8 million at the box office, an unprecedented record) have appeared on the *Variety* charts alongside major American hits, and Quebec features — such as Manon Briand's *La turbulence des fluides*, André Turpin's *Une crabe dans la tête*, Denis Villeneuve's *Maelstrom*, and Denis Chouinard's *L'ange du Goudron* — are running on a regular basis in the theatres. In 2003, I was especially happy to see a filmmaker whom the CFDC had supported from the early days (*La maudite galette* –1972) triumph at the Cannes Film Festival. Denys Arcand won the best screenplay award for

AGAINST ALL ODDS (1995 ONWARDS)

215

Les invasions barbares just as the box-office in Quebec reached $1 million. Marie-José Croze also garnered the award for best actress.

Denise Robert has followed in the footsteps of Pierre Lamy, becoming an outstanding entrepreneur of the Quebec feature film industry. As the CFDC (and then Telefilm) always said, the industry must have both an entrepreneurial and an artistic base to succeed. The idea proposed to Guy Roberge by Quebec filmmakers in the corridors of the NFB in the 1960s has, in fact, come to fruition. It has taken forty years, but we now have a Quebec feature film industry that's here to stay.

We had started out with the idea that a government loan fund was all that was needed to launch a Canadian feature film industry. The interdepartmental committee had reached the conclusion in 1964 that the industry would produce enough profitable features every year to support itself on a continuing basis. Believing in the rightness of our cause, we had managed to convince the government that it would only need to come up with $10 million once, and the industry would be on its feet forever. But this industry is also an art, as Malraux said. Today, far from running on its own, the industry receives subsidies of over $300 million each year from Canadian taxpayers. This is the price of keeping Canadian culture alive — and it's worth every penny. Who could ever have imagined that the original $10 million would grow to support an industry (and an art) worth more than $3 billion a year?

AGAINST ALL ODDS (1995 ONWARDS)

ACKNOWLEDGEMENTS

My original inspiration to write this book came from my grand-uncle, George Croal (1811-1907). A journalist in Edinburgh, Scotland, his *Living Memories of an Octogenarian* was published in 1874, when he was 83. I brought my mother's dog-eared copy of it in the 'Settler's Effects' that the Canadian government allowed me to import to Canada duty free as a landed immigrant. When I came across it many years later, I naturally assumed that I should follow a family tradition.

Once I began to work on a history of the Canadian feature film industry, I was given access to the files of the Canadian Film Development Corporation by François Macerola, the executive director at the time. It was he who suggested that Suzan Ayscough would be an ideal collaborator, considering her experience as a journalist, especially during the 80s when I was no longer at the centre of events. I accepted this proposal enthusiastically and I wish to express my thanks to both of them. It would be fair to say that this book could not have been written without their assistance.

A book needs a publisher and it was Jean-Claude Mahé who first proposed that we discuss our ideas with Pierre Turgeon of Éditions Trait d'union. As the work progressed (and I did indeed begin in 1999), Pierre expanded his activities into English Canada and launched Cantos books across the country.

In the meantime Natasha Hall had come to work as my assistant and together we spent many weeks sending the text back and forth between Montreal and Toronto until we had satisfied the high standards of clarity and style required by the publishing house. I am immensely grateful to Karen Alliston, Donna Brown, and Natasha for their patience and understanding during this period. Natasha was also very skilful when it came to using the computer for research. I would have been totally lost without her expertise.

I would also like to thank our translator, George Tombs, as well as Cantos' associate publisher Andrea Gourgy and the rest of the CTU team who made sure the book went to press.

A major element in a history of this kind is the interview. I should like to thank Denys Arcand, David Cronenberg, Marc Daigle, Pierre David, Rock Demers, John Dunning, Hugh Faulkner, Michèle Favreau, Francis Fox, Stephen Greenberg, Harry Gulkin, Denis Héroux, Donald Johnston, Robert Lantos, Carole Langlois, Jean-Pierre Lefebvre, Ronald Legault, André Link, François Macerola, Michael MacMillan, Danielle Ouimet, David Perlmutter, Donald Pilon, Larry Pilon, Christian Rasselet, John Roberts, Millard Roth, Ted Rouse and Gil Taylor. All of them submitted to recorded interviews with me and/or Suzan Ayscough. In addition I had conversations with Sid Adilman, Lionel Chetwynd, John Kemeny, Arnold Kopelson, Micheline Lanctôt, Flora MacDonald, Judith McCann, Mickey Stevenson and Eric Till. I take full responsibility if my memory has failed to record precisely what they said. An earlier draft was read by Royce Frith, Kirwan Cox and Wyndham Wise. I thank them for their comments.

I owe special thanks to Carole Laure and Donald Sutherland, whose forewords are printed in both the English and French versions. Finally, Richard Stursberg has continued François Macerola's support of the project for which I thank him but I emphasize again that this is my version of events. Not an official history.

AKNOWLEDGEMENTS

INDEX OF NAMES

ABOUT THE AUTHORS

Michael Spencer

A member of the Canadian Army's Feature Film Photo Unit during World War II, Michael Spencer has been fascinated with celluloid (and birds) for decades. Little did he know that when he was a top planning executive at the National Film Board of Canada -- crafting a friendly little two-page memo to Cabinet -- that he would be helping change the feature film scene in Canada forever. Michael Spencer was one of the founders of the Canadian Film Development Corporation in 1967 and served as its first executive director until 1978. Known today as Telefilm Canada, Michael is still familiar with the Crown Corporation's film and television activities in his role as a bonder for Film Finances Canada. Michael Spencer was awarded the Order of Canada in 1989.

Suzan Ayscough

A 1982 film school graduate from Ottawa's Carleton University, Suzan is a veteran of the Canadian film and TV landscape. Suzan has had a front-row seat as both a critic and participant in the private and public film and television sectors in Canada and the U.S. She began her film career in Montreal in the early 80s as a film critic and reporter for *Daily Variety* then moved to Los Angeles for *Variety* in 1991. She joined Canada's private sector back in Montreal in 1993 as head of communications for Cinar and then subsequently became the vice president for Alliance Communications in Toronto. Suzan then became Telefilm Canada's director of Communications, Public Affairs & Festivals for five years. Today Suzan is a communications consultant and writer.

CANADIAN CINEMA 101 (1945-1964)